Foundations for a Humanitarian Economy

The modern global economy and discipline of economics place mathematical calculation above human concern. However, a re-reading of Boethius' *The Consolation of Philosophy* can positively highlight the contrast in values and spirit of the early medieval European world with our own scientific age.

The book discusses the historical and cultural contexts that influenced Boethius' writing and explores how *Consolation* offers a radically different understanding of economic concepts: wealth from inner happiness and virtues, poverty from hoarding outer possessions, self-sufficiency in the greater whole, enlightenment through misfortune, and development as fruition from the Good. These economic considerations resonate with a range of heterodox economic perspectives, such as Ecological and Buddhist Economics. The fundamental revaluations gained through Boethius pose a critique of mainstream neoclassical and neoliberal economics: to consumerism, avarice, growth and technology fetishism, and market rationality. These economic foundations resonate into a time when global crises raise the question of fundamental human priorities, offering alternatives to an ever-expanding industrial market economy designed for profit, and helping to avoid irrevocable socio-ecological disasters.

The issues raised and questioned in this book will be of significant interest to readers with concern for pluralist approaches to economics, philosophy, classics, ancient history, and theology.

William D. Bishop is an independent scholar. Born in London in 1945, he pursued a career largely in telecommunications before studying for degrees in the History and Theory of Art. His MA at the University of Wales at Aberystwyth included a dissertation on WH Fox Talbot, the English inventor and practitioner of an early paper-based photographic process. This led to freelance writing: exhibition reviews and photography features particularly as a regular contributor to the *British Journal of Photography* (1982–1992).

As a publisher and editor, he launched a small-scale quarterly journal for independent photographers, *Inscape* magazine, in 1991. The fruit of which was a self-published book in 1997: *Realising Personal Truths in Photography*, Inscape, London. Career activities include work in the British Library and the specialist library at Rudolf Steiner House in London. Besides some memoir-related books published through the online publisher, Lulu Press, his interest in writing and philosophy merged into association with 'The Wednesday' group, and several of his articles in recent years appear in *The Wednesday*.

Economics and Humanities

Series Editor: Sebastian Berger

University of the West of England (UWE Bristol), UK

The *Economics and Humanities* series presents the economic wisdom of the humanities and arts. Its volumes gather the economic senses sheltered and revealed by some of the most excellent sources within philosophy, poetry, art, and story-telling. By re-rooting economics in its original domain these contributions allow economic phenomena and their meanings to come into the open more fully; indeed, they allow us to ask anew the question "What is economics?". Economic truth is thus shown to arise from the Human rather than the Market.

Readers will gain a foundational understanding of a humanities-based economics and find their economic sensibility enriched. They should turn to this series if they are interested in questions such as: What are the economic consequences of rooting economic Truth in the Human? What is the purpose of a humanities-based economics? What is the proper meaning of the 'oikos', and how does it arise? What are the true meanings of wealth and poverty, gain and loss, capital and productivity? In what sense is economic reasoning with words more fundamental than reasoning with numbers? What is the dimension and measure of human dwelling in the material world?

These volumes address themselves to all those who are interested in sources and foundations for economic wisdom. Students and academics who are fundamentally dissatisfied with the state of economics and worried that its crisis undermines society will find this series of interest.

Economics, Accounting and the True Nature of Capitalism
Capitalism, Ecology and Democracy
Jacques Richard and Alexandre Rambaud

Foundations for a Humanitarian Economy
Re-thinking Boethius' *Consolation of Philosophy*
William D. Bishop

For more information about this series, please visit: www.routledge.com/Economics-and-Humanities/book-series/RSECH

Foundations for a Humanitarian Economy

Re-thinking Boethius' *Consolation of Philosophy*

William D. Bishop

First published 2022
by Routledge
4 Park Square, Milton Park, Abingdon, Oxon OX14 4RN

and by Routledge
605 Third Avenue, New York, NY 10158

Routledge is an imprint of the Taylor & Francis Group, an informa business

British Library Cataloguing-in-Publication Data
A catalogue record for this book is available from the British Library

Library of Congress Cataloging-in-Publication Data
Names: Bishop, William D., 1945– author.
Title: Foundations for a humanitarian economy : re-thinking Boethius' *Consolation of philosophy* / William D. Bishop.
Description: Abingdon, Oxon ; New York, NY : Routledge, 2022. | Series: Economics and humanities | Includes bibliographical references and index.
Identifiers: LCCN 2021059443 | ISBN 9781032127583 (hbk) | ISBN 9781032127620 (pbk) | ISBN 9781003226093 (ebk)
Subjects: LCSH: Boethius, -524. De consolatione philosophiae.
Classification: LCC B659.D473 B49 2022 | DDC 189—dc23/eng/20220218
LC record available at https://lccn.loc.gov/2021059443

ISBN: 978-1-032-12758-3 (hbk)
ISBN: 978-1-032-12762-0 (pbk)
ISBN: 978-1-003-22609-3 (ebk)

DOI: 10.4324/9781003226093

Contents

Acknowledgement

Special thanks to Dr. Sebastian Berger for his constructive expertise in this heterodox approach to an economy for human flourishing.

1 Introduction

The Consolation of Philosophy presents ideas for the good life that are relevant to re-thinking economics. The economy it presents is that of the soul, which is the home of the Human, the 'oikos'. Traditionally, the soul is the region of activity that connects the earthly with the divine: with what is in time and what is beyond time. As an intermediary, it takes on a 'higher' and a 'lower' aspect because of its interface with the divine (spirit) and the earthly (body). In terms of life on the earth, the soul is essentially the identity of a person resident in a material body. The soul is the pertinent home of a person; therefore, the oikos (as the household economy) applies to the soul, and essentially the oikos here is concerned with human welfare.

At the commonly regarded beginning of 'modern philosophy', Descartes (1596–1650) made a distinction between soul and body (spirit and matter), and consequently this decisive separation became accepted so that spirit and matter have become regarded as quite distinct and separate regions, or alternatively the material world of the empirical senses has been accepted as the only real world. Prior to Descartes, tradition regarded the soul as the connection between spirit and body, and the living human being was regarded as a unity of spirit–soul–body. The oikos, as Soul, therefore takes economic account of both spirit and body and not only material concerns.

Facing death, Boethius, tormented in soul, engages in a dialogue with Philosophia (the divine personification of philosophy) who guides him towards sorely needed consolation. At the heart of *Consolation* is the mysterious economy of the soul that yields understanding, fruition, and fulfilment. This is an economy based on a combination of reason as logic and the liberal art of poetry. Reason complemented by poetry combines mind (spirit) and soul, which constitutes the power of poetry and philosophy to reveal Truth. Such a poetic economy does not mean abandoning Truth or reason. Poetry is unique in its combination of imagination, intuition, and artistic insight, and in the way that it links ideas through reflection.

DOI: 10.4324/9781003226093-1

The literary form of *The Consolation* is that of Menippean satire, an alternation of prose and verse. In the opening metre, Boethius says that previously he had written songs with pleasure. However, the poetry in *Consolation* functions to complement and balance the logic of the prose dialogue. Two of the books written by Boethius, which were influential during the medieval age, were *On Mathematics* and *On Music*. Here, the apparent dichotomy between logic and art was not compartmentalized in the mind of Boethius in the way that this might be for a modern person. For him, the mind and soul complemented each other in the search for Truth. Boethius had the mind of a philosopher, the heart of a Romantic, and the soul of a Platonist (Harpur, 2007: 14).

Boethius was nourished particularly by Plato's artistic and rational consciousness and Aristotle's scientific and logical mind that regarded reason as the ground for knowledge. However, he also valued intuition and the ideas of Plotinus (c. 205–270), many of which relate to mystical union with the One, a form of experiential knowledge that is supra-rational and intellectual in nature.[1] There is also an underlying Stoic element, and yet for Boethius, it seems that God was the Father God that has will and intention for the world and humanity. Knowledge for Boethius was not based on thought alone but on religious revelation and reflection and intuition. He was able to balance Aristotle's soul in the process of cognition, becoming all things (intentionally) with the Platonic conception of the soul as a microcosm of the macrocosmic 'World Soul'.

In terms of harmonious balance, Iain McGilchrist's cognitive theory is worth considering (McGilchrist, 2009). Here, the right hemisphere of the brain takes in the whole living experience, while the left hemisphere processes the details and *re-presents* the experience. So, on the one hand, there is knowledge in the *process of becoming* that involves participation, and on the other, what is experienced becomes a *thing* in a subject–object relationship. If this is so, then language (logic) as a left hemisphere function, and song (music) that engages the right hemisphere, creates a perfect cognitive harmony within Boethius' *Consolation of Philosophy*, with its interrelated text and song. This can be interpreted as harmony between mind and soul (reason and feeling).

A key idea in *Consolation* is that the human being is made in the image of God. God is the 'hinge' and still point of the turning world. This image of the circle (and circular flow) is a central theme, which is also embodied in the structure of the composition with its primal prayer to God as its central turning point. As the Soul circles the mind of God, and centres of concentric circles coincide, so there is interaction between God and the human soul, with God as the Good and life's motivation. The equation – soul equals oikos – casts the economy in a special light and reveals its fundamental difference from modern neoclassical and neoliberal economics. *Consolation*'s presentation of the significance of the soul and mind (spirit) and the dignity of human nature emphasize the need for a human-centred economy. Here, the idea of fruition[2] is raised where the part is vitalized in its relation to the whole. In this respect, the *Consolation* provides a fresh economic logic much needed at a time when today's economy, with its global and technological interconnections, has become so complex that it undermines, rather than supports, general welfare. The ethical stance and clarity with which *Consolation* identifies human nature supply a different understanding of the economy, one that nourishes and consoles. H. M. Barrett observed that in *The Religion of Time and the Religion of Eternity* (Wickstead, 1899), Wickstead suggested that modern civilization had tended to cultivate a religion of Time rather than a religion of Eternity, and had stressed *Progress* rather than *Fruition* and so had lost the conception of a goal, of a life supremely worth living for its own sake, and with this had lost the meaning of Progress as an ever-growing experience of that supreme life (Barrett, 1940: 136).

Consolation equates the Good with happiness, which everyone seeks, but too often is sought along false paths, and the assertion is made that by participating in the Good, a person redeems their divinity. Man has to negotiate the Wheel of earthly Fortune, and through virtue and self-control and balance between extremes, is able to achieve a state of beatitude: the Good. The *Consolation* therefore promotes a vision of the Good for society, with the corollary of justice, morality, and ethical values. In its application to economics, it is these values that form the foundation for the economy. W. P. Ker once remarked that Boethius was a seeker after a vision where the moral nature should be regenerated, and the goodness of man is shown to maintain the universe. For Ker, the message in the *Consolation* on which all depends is an affirmation of what Plato said in the *Timaeus* that there are two kinds of causes, the Divine and the Necessary, and we must seek for the Divine in all things, and the Necessary for the sake of the Divine (Ker, 1923/1955: 108).

The Greek, Roman, and medieval economy were embedded in society and acknowledged a spiritual dimension to life. This was later eclipsed by a materialistic model, which dethroned God. This different orientation enabled a market economy, and later a market society, to dominate life, which then only becomes comprehensible in terms of calculation and price as exchange value (Varoufakis, 2017: 38). Here, the profit motive turns money from a means into an end, so that the essential idea of the oikos is disregarded. This allows commodity exchange value to rise above experiential value. For instance, if environmental qualities have no exchange value, then the market calculus ignores them. The economist, Yanis Varoufakis, contends that if we are to have any chance of saving the planet and ourselves today, we must find ingenious ways to reactivate humanity's appreciation for experiential values that no market can even recognize or respect (Varoufakis, 2017: 173). Human well-being depends on having a planet on which to thrive, and the sustainability of the planet depends very much on having a necessary and experiential economy as indicated in the *Consolation* of Boethius.

In his study of the history of economics, Niall Kishtainy concluded that our contemporary world needs to return to the broader questions of the philosophers of Ancient Greece who first thought about economics by asking what it takes to live well in human society; what people need to be happy and fulfilled; and what makes people truly thrive (Kishtainy, 2017: 241). These are the very questions that *Consolation* addresses to an economy that has 'wandered away' from its fundamental role of serving society, and in doing so, hinders the prospects of people to thrive and survive in society. For Boethius, a thriving life demanded excellence: the ability to activate the Good, and through virtue, to fulfil the potential of human nature.[3] For Aristotle, 'Eudaimonia' was the state of flourishing.[4] That such happiness is possible within and through the oikos is Boethius' message to us today living on the same planet but in a very different world.

This book is organized in such a way that it initially presents the context in which *The Consolation of Philosophy* was written, and it then introduces the author, Boethius, within his historical setting. This is followed by a detailed summary of the dramatic dialogue of the *Consolation*. Then, it follows an examination of the separate themes in the light of the contribution that the *Consolation* can make to economics today. A concluding chapter defines ten relevant insights, and proposes ideas and strategies for creating a humanitarian economy on the basis of the oikos as a model adapted to function in our contemporary world. Reasons are also given for the need of a fresh vision for society, which will affect economics.

Notes

1 Plato and Plotinus differentiated between reason (*dianoia*), and intellect (*nous*) that is direct, intellectual perception. Cf. H.J. Sleeman and G. Pollet, *Lexicon Plotinianum*. Leiden: Brill, 1980, 244–245, 677–684.
2 This is also an Augustinian concept. Cf. the opposition between *uti* (good as a means to something else) and *frui* (good in itself).
3 This is possible when someone has the right hierarchy of values and seeks for the real good within their reach.
4 Aristotle said that happiness is at once the most beautiful and best of all things. *The Eudemian Ethics of Aristotle*. London: Routledge, 2017, 1214a6–1214a7.

References

Aristotle (2017). *The Eudemian Ethics of Aristotle*. Translated by Peter L.P. Simpson. London: Routledge.

Barrett, H.M. (1940). *Boethius: Some Aspects of His Times and Work*. Cambridge: Cambridge University Press.

Harpur, J. (2007). *Boethius – Fortune's Prisoner*. London: Anvil Press Poetry.

Ker, W.P. (1923/1955). *The Dark Ages*. London: Thomas Nelson & Sons.

Kishtainy, Niall (2017). *A Little History of Economics*. New Haven: Yale University Press.

McGilchrist, Iain (2009). *The Master and His Emissary: The Divided Brain and the Making of the Western World*. New Haven and London: Yale University Press.

Sleeman, H.J. and Pollet, G. (1980). *Lexicon Plotinianum*. Leiden: Brill.

Varoufakis, Yanis (2017). *Talking to My Daughter About the Economy*. London: Bodley Head.

Wickstead, Philip Henry (1899/1932). *The Religion of Time and the Religion of Eternity.* London: P. Green. London: Lindsey Press (1932) .

2 The Consolation in Context

a. Historical Background

Boethius was born at a time and place where Neoplatonism flourished. Plotinus, its founder, taught in Rome from 244 until his death in 270, while Boethius was born in Rome five years before the death of its last major philosopher, Proclus, who died in Athens in 485.[1]

In the year 324, Constantine became sole Roman Emperor. He adopted Christianity and established Constantinople as a second capital of the empire. Following him, the emperor Julian (called by Christians the Apostate) tried to re-establish Paganism. After his death, the emperor Theodosius (reigned 379–392) established Christianity as the empire's official religion. St. Augustine of Hippo in North Africa died in 430 just when Proclus was settling into Athens to pursue for the next 50 years his version of Neoplatonism. St. Augustine, who profoundly influenced Christian thought, had been converted to Christianity after ten years as a member of the Manicheans and attachment to Neoplatonism.

Attila, leading an invading force of Huns from Mongolia, left incredible devastation in his wake, but after the middle of the fifth century, the danger of Mongolian conquest of the West was averted. By then, the territories of Gaul, Spain, Africa, and Britain had seceded from Roman rule, which radically reduced the size of the Roman Empire. Invasions of the empire by barbarians, including the Goths, over many years resulted eventually in cooperation between the Romans and Goths led by Odoacer. Released from compulsion to serve the warring interests of the Huns, Theodoric, king of the Ostrogoths (Eastern Goths) led his people over the Alps into Italy and after defeating Odoacer, who had originally displaced the previous Western Roman Emperor, took his place by murdering him in 493. The Goths, a wandering people, were ready to settle and Theoderic settled his people into a third of Italy. As the king of the Ostrogoths, based in Ravenna, he was effectively Viceroy to the Emperor in Constantinople, so he was effectively

DOI: 10.4324/9781003226093-2

ruler of the western territory. This was the political situation into which Boethius was born within imperial Rome in 480.

The Goths lived alongside the Romans under Roman law and provided the military force of the region. The Ostrogoths were Christians but subscribed to the 'Arian heresy', which considered the Father and Son not to be of the same substance. This contradicted the orthodox papal view that the Father and Son have equality within the Divine Trinity. Boethius had written pamphlets in support of the Pope's official view, and when in 519 the Emperor Justin initiated the submission of Constantinople, as the eastern capital, to Rome (as the western capital) and began persecution of Arians in the East, Theodoric must have feared for suppression of the Gothic partnership in the empire. With his political allegiance to Theodoric and his spiritual allegiance to the Pope, Boethius found himself in a situation of divided loyalty. This led to his downfall when accused of sacrilege and treason. For his part, although coming to office through violence, Theodoric had ruled peacefully for 30 years and had restored prosperity to the region previously devastated by the invaders. He encouraged agriculture so that corn and wine were plentiful. Under his reign, marshes were drained, mining established, and buildings restored, including drains in Rome and aqueducts in Ravenna (Barrett, 1940: 29).

b. Boethius

Anicius Manlius Severinus Boethius was born around the year 480 into an ancient aristocratic Roman family, the 'gens Anicia', recognized for their public service and conversion to Christianity in the fourth century. After his father's death when Boethius was a boy, he became a ward of the celebrated house of Symmachus, where he was encouraged to pursue his love of scholarship.

It is likely that Theodoric first met Boethius on his six-month-long visit to Rome in 1500 when Boethius was 20. Subsequently, Theodoric gave Boethius commissions, which may have later drawn him into official office (Barrett, 1940: 45). In fact, under Theodoric, Boethius became Consul in 510 (an office traditionally held for one year), and in 522, his two sons were jointly made Consuls and he was appointed Head of the Civil Service and the Senate. Yet within a year, he was condemned to death with the approval of Theodoric and the Senate. It was in the interval between his confinement at Ticenum and his execution that he wrote *The Consolation of Philosophy*.

Born into a respected ancient family in the capital city of a vast empire and cared for by a foster father who encouraged him in scholarship, Boethius was well placed to satisfy his hunger for knowledge. He was an earnest student engaged with the *quadrivium*, comprising arithmetic, geometry, astronomy, and music, and what later became known as the *trivium* of grammar, rhetoric, and dialectic. These were adopted as the seven liberal arts of the medieval curriculum. Boethius also composed texts and his translations of Aristotle's works on logic (the *Organon*)[2] were of immense value during the Middle Ages as was his translation of Porphyry's *Isagogue* (an introduction to Aristotle's Categories). His handbooks on arithmetic and music (*Institutio arithmetica, Institutio musica*) were standard manuals throughout the Middle Ages, but arguably his most influential work has been *The Consolation of Philosophy*. This has given readers through the ages spiritual consolation within a beautiful world and yet rife with injustice and suffering.

The Roman world was deeply influenced by Greek culture to the extent that it can be said that Rome conquered Greece but Greek culture conquered Rome. During the early imperial period, Roman aristocracy spoke Greek, but this declined so that in the later stages of the disintegrating empire into which Boethius was born, Greek philosophy required translation into Latin. It was Boethius' deep love for Greek culture and philosophy that inspired him to want to communicate this rich heritage to his fellow Romans. His care for the soul derived from his devotion to the Platonic tradition and to Aristotelian, Stoic, and Neoplatonic philosophy in addition to notable Roman literature, and Christianity. It is against the background of these sources that the *Consolation* situates the identity, origin, and destination of the human being, and determines the nature of the consolation that is sought. Boethius' actual comments on the economy therefore originate from a perspective that values a person as a *soul* in relation to a divine whole.

Banished 500 miles from his home, with a death sentence pending, Boethius consoles himself with philosophy and draws on his accumulated knowledge to assure himself about his true home, both in time and beyond. His reflections, backed by logic and song, in effect create a Theodicy: a vindication of divine justice in the righteous government of the universe in the face of moral anarchy and evil and the suffering of the innocent.

In the *Consolation*, Boethius has created a text that can be taken as a guide for living a virtuous life oriented towards the Good and rewarded by happiness. Importantly, it is the moral values that he presents with clarity that equally apply to the economy. Ideas of mortality and eternity were a live issue for Boethius at the time he was writing the *Consolation* and this must undoubtedly have influenced the urgency in his assessment and attitude to life and Being, and the relevant place of the oikos to the soul as home in these considerations.

For Plato, the Idea as *Form* was the enduring reality, and in contrast, ideas for Aristotle were at home in the mind and in things. In retrospect, it is possible to see that an era can be dominated by an overriding idea where, for instance, the Form of *theocracy* provides structure for an ancient civilized world until replaced by city-states of Greece with their political forms, one of which was *democracy*. Here, an *idea* becomes grounded in reality. The idea names the form in reality and its manifestation as appearance reveals its Form. This represents Realism in contrast to Nominalism where a name merely represents a concept. In the medieval period, there was a great debate regarding these two conceptions, which ended in favour of Nominalism. This then led European civilization in a particular direction. However, in relation to ideas that relate to reality, Boethius' *The Consolation of Philosophy* is a drama that raises the question for us today of how these ideas that he presents serve us to rethink economics by re-rooting our understanding of the economy in the humanities.

It is worth remarking on similarity between Boethius and Plato that can only increase the significance of Boethius for us. Both were philosophers with a concern for theology and morality; both had a wide breadth of interest; and both wrote philosophy as literature (at least *The Consolation* in the case of Boethius). It is interesting in this respect that Boethius' studies led to translating work and commentaries, particularly in philosophy concerned with the idea of the *Good*. However, it is ironic that in trying to live a good life, inspired by reading Plato's *Republic*, Boethius had entered public service and by acting ethically had made enemies who later, as he says, bore false witness against him, forcing him into the situation of seclusion from which he composed *The Consolation*. Apart from any consolation that the work brought to him, it became highly influential, celebrated, and valued during the medieval period and beyond. Knowledge of the *essential* nature of man and *awareness* of divine presence have largely been lost in our time, and are therefore not taken seriously into account in the world of politics and economics, but this *perennial philosophy* presented by Boethius, with its logical and poetic presentation, maintains significant relevance for us today.

c. Philosophy's 'Consolation'

Banished 500 miles from Rome to Ticenum (modern Pavia), Boethius' confinement provided space and time for intensely concentrated reflection and recollection. He was able to review his life and ideas, and importantly, to establish a connection between the world of time and eternity. This gave him perspective on his dire position with his earthly time running out. Immanent death concentrates the mind, and the thoughts that emerge in the *Consolation* resolve his perplexity, leading to the prospect of inner peace of mind, and even present happiness. It was Stoic 'medicinal' practice to act upon oneself with thinking to gain consolation in a difficult situation when nothing could be done about it,[3] and the fundamentally Platonic philosophy that Boethius draws upon is a unified view where recollection and reason conclude with the idea of the *Good* as a unifying aim in life, a telos: a Good that unites beauty and truth with love as its executive power binding all together.

Although a tradition of '*consolatio*' existed, it is likely that the intense circumstances in which Boethius wrote his own 'consolation' allowed him to bring to this genre a special *sobriety*, *urgency*, and *authenticity*.[4] He must have experienced the acute existential need to find the Truth of his being within reality, and so turned towards his memorized resources of philosophy and poetry. Traditionally, philosophy has been the 'love of wisdom' (and the desire to live it) and the wisdom that Boethius was drawn to must be distinguished from modern theology as a distinct discipline, for in his day philosophical wisdom included the divine world that was seen to encompass the human world, so that theology and philosophy were understood within the unity of philosophy's vision, although theology was regarded as the highest part of speculative philosophy.[5]

An essential concern of *The Consolation* is the True home of the human: that still centre amid time and change. The text employs recollection with the desire to achieve self-possession and ownership of this 'home'. The title of Boethius' book suggests that the consolation provided by the goddess Philosophia is medicine for his soul, and it can equally be understood as consolation *from* philosophy for anyone who needs it. Boethius may have had this joint motive in mind. Also the urgency linked to the death sentence must have focused Boethius' mind sharply enough to achieve a breakthrough to illumination through appraising his philosophical knowledge. Indeed, when (in imagination) Philosophia enters Boethius' cell, that is the moment when he gains the prospect where illumination could outshine the prospect of death.[6] From then on, he is able to dramatize his reflections in a Platonic dialogue within the discipline of an established literary form.

The Consolation of Philosophy can also be interpreted as a dialogue between the Self and the soul,[7] an *economy* of the soul, an impassioned and scholarly testament concerning his soul in its earthly predicament situated between the material world and a divine eternity. Indeed, the *Consolation* discusses some of the fundamental dilemmas facing humanity. Written as it was by a Roman citizen at a critical time of political and religious sensitivity within a crumbling empire, its timeless and universal appeal is primarily due to its profound synthesis and presentation of Greek philosophy in combination with quotations from the literature and poetry of the ancient world. The creative and imaginative tone in the writing of Boethius adds drama to the underlying Stoic philosophy that was intended to fortify the human spirit in the face of life's inner trials and changes of fortune.[8]

As a necessary work arising from a condition of extremity, the *Consolation* includes strong feeling in its logical dialogue and plain logic in its poetry.[9] Its message is that it is possible to face life with a sense of completion while embedded in passing time. Completion refers to the whole, to eternity, to which there is immanent connection. For Boethius here, as also for Plotinus and St. Augustine, the possibility of the experience of simultaneous awareness of living within time and a transcendent world must have meant inhabiting a qualitatively rich reality.

Boethius deferred much to Plato who in the *Laws* determined God's moral government of the world through 'natural theology'.[10] Although Boethius was a Christian, in this his final composition, he relies on philosophy for consolation, arguably because he wants a logical argument that could provide reasoned certainty.[11] That must explain why he refers to God without mentioning Christ, and yet a Christian sensibility underpins the work. Boethius' God in the *Consolation* is essentially the monotheistic Father God and at the same time the pre-Christian God of the philosophers. Because reason is at the heart of the *Consolation*, this invites the view that Boethius was the last of the Roman philosophers and the first of the scholastic theologians. Indeed, it is because of Boethius' relatively simple and direct expression in his philosophical synthesis that the educator W. P. Ker commented that the task that Boethius set himself was philosophical consolation rather than pure philosophy (Ker, 1923/1955: 114). In fact, *Consolation*'s synthesis of ratio, logic, and poetry arguably creates a balanced philosophy of reasoned poetics that reconciles faith with reason.[12]

Boethius had expressed an intention to reconcile Aristotle with Plato at a fundamental level,[13] and in the light of this, he presumably saw no gulf between 'pagan' philosophy and Christianity, unlike the Roman Emperor Justinian, who feared that 'pagan' philosophy would distance Roman citizens from Christianity. Consequently, in the year 529, five years after the execution of Boethius, he ordered the closure of all the remaining philosophy schools in Athens.

In extremity, it appears to be second nature for a person to call on God, which suggests that recognition of divinity is instinctive and not just a question of philosophy or theology. Acknowledgement of divinity may appear to be academic in the way that arguments are presented with logical precision in the *Consolation* (as medicine to restore the memory of the true human home), and yet the sense is conveyed that Boethius had a deeply felt belief in the divine world because sincerity and depth of feeling palpably inform the content and craft of his text.

While Plato brought Pythagorean ideas and myth into a rational context, Boethius integrates Plato with the ethics of Aristotle, the morality of the Stoics, and the mysticism of Plotinus and Protagoras. In achieving this, Boethius' *Consolation* represents an imaginative and personalized synthesis of knowledge embodied as spiritual nourishment and love for wisdom and Truth as far as such knowledge was possible then. Indeed, according to the historian of philosophy, Pierre Hadot, Neoplatonism became an original synthesis of Plato with Aristotelianism and Stoicism (Hadot, 1995: 56). The rationale behind the consolation in *The Consolation of Philosophy* can be determined from remarks made by Boethius in a commentary on Porphyry where he said in effect that the love of wisdom in philosophy enlightens the intelligent mind by the wisdom of the pure living mind and primeval reason of all things, investing the different classes of minds with its divinity as well as restoring a pure nature and rightly orientated constitution.[14]

The powerful nature of *Consolation* is therefore made manifest through Boethius' dramatization of the text, which includes the alternation of prose with lyric poetry in combination with a synthesis of ancient wisdom and personal involvement in the dialogue. The silence from Boethius as a character in the final section of the *Consolation*, where the text becomes a monologue by Philosophia, suggests a transformation in Boethius through the light of understanding: beatitude in preparation for a good death. Reason and logic alone are not sufficient to influence the will. The will is affected by emotion, so in trying to persuade himself, Boethius alternates logic with song (music) to produce persuasive argument supplemented with emotional force. What concerns *Consolation* is the establishment of a right and just relationship to reality, with its associated peace of mind and sense of wholeness. Boethius immersed himself in his studies to such an extent that he was able to reflect their substance as of living consequence and relevance to the human in relation to Nature and Divinity. He encapsulated this in *Consolation* in a deliberate literary form that progressively dramatizes his growing insight and sense of completion in union with the whole.

d. Reception and Influence

It wasn't until the late eighth century that the *Consolation* became more widely known. This resulted from a commentary by Alcuin of York (Nauta in Marenbon, 2009: 257). It was then read widely in monasteries and Cathedral schools within the Carolingian Empire, and then commentaries and glosses became common with their clarifications, explanations, and background information to allusions in the text. By this means, the *Consolation* became a central text within Europe until the end of the medieval period. It has been described as a bestseller for 1,000 years (Patch,

1935), and was instrumental in forming a new European culture at a time of transition from the crumbling Roman Empire to a culture dominated by Christianity.

One of the earliest translations from Latin into the vernacular was made in the late ninth century into Old English under the direction of the Anglo-Saxon king, Alfred. His translation replaced the combination of text and poetry with 42 chapters, and Lady Philosophy became Wisdom and Reason. Since the object behind this translation was to revive learning and Christian morality, extra material was included with enthusiasm. According to H. F. Stewart, Alfred envisioned the city of Truth, from which Boethius is exiled, becoming the heavenly Jerusalem, and Christ as the haven of quiet to which the wise man turns for shelter from the storms of life (Stewart, 1891: 177).

The tenth-century translation by Notker, at the monastery of St. Gall, included the Latin text along with High German and glosses in the vernacular closely following the text. This was intended for study in schools and monasteries. Similarly, the eleventh-century Provençal poem, *Boece*, on the life of Boethius, was intended as moral instruction and encouragement to live a holy life in difficult times.

In the late ninth century, the monk, Bovo of Corvey, declared Boethius' ideas to be 'monstrous comments' and that the Platonic doctrines were nothing but 'most inane fables', and that the *Consolation* was often 'contrary to faith' (Nauta in Marenbon, 2009: 259). Alfred too had complained of having to use classical fables rather than biblical stories (Wetherbee in Marenbon, 2009: 280). So at this early stage in its history, there was a definite distinction drawn between Christianity and paganism. Yet in the thirteenth century, William of Conches declared that there is nothing superfluous in such a perfect work as the *Consolation* written by such a perfect philosopher as Boethius. William of Conches was also the first commentator to give a fair synopsis, adding arguments from natural philosophy to support Boethius' reliance on Plato's cosmology (Nauta in Marenbon, 2009: 260–261). Around the year 1300, in its preface to Philip IV, Jean de Meun's translation claimed that the *Consolatio*n had value as a guide for distinguishing true from false goods.

Just how Christian the work is has been a matter of debate. The later medieval period that included theologians such as Thomas Aquinas tended to accept the pagan aspect as being in harmony with Christianity, making it appear that earlier theologians were inclined to dogmatism and were highly sensitive to 'heresy'. Two influential works of twelfth-century Latin literature can be read as rewritings of the *Consolation*: the *Cosmographia* of Bernardus Silvestris (1147) and *De Planctu Naturae* of Alan of Lille (1160–70) (Wetherbee in Marenbon, 2009: 280). Rewritings such as these emphasize the significance of the work.

In the fourteenth century, the commentary by the Dominican, Nicholas Trevet (c. 1300) became the most respected late medieval commentary, representing a non-dogmatic defence of Boethius' text which supported its underlying Platonism. The use of fables was accepted in the traditional manner where fables signify deeper truths that are otherwise hard to express in language. Written during the 1380s, Chaucer's Middle English, *Boece*, attends closely to the original Latin. Here, Boethius' idea of the tragedy of Fortune influenced Chaucer's *Troilus and Criseyde* and *The Knight's Tale*, both of which were written around the time of Chaucer's translation of the *Consolation*. Another interesting reception of Boethius' work is to be found in two works by Christine de Pisan (1364–1430): *City of Ladies* and *Livre de la Mutation de Fortune*.

William of Aragon's commentary, which possibly predates that of Trevet, interprets Boethius as being more of an Aristotelian than a Platonist. However, since Boethius expressed his desire to reconcile Aristotle and Plato, it seems that he attempts to bridge the two, giving equal prominence to Aristotle's logic and Plato's metaphysics. However, a Neoplatonic influence in the *Consolation* must not be underestimated, nor an implicit Christian orientation. The Dutch commentator, Joannes Murmellius, in his work published in 1514 in the manner of a humanist grammar teacher, accepted most of Boethius' Platonic doctrines without the need to Christianize them (Nauta in Marenbon, 2009: 272). And interestingly, Leibniz summarized books One and Two, and wrote that a friend of his had affection for the *Consolation* because he traced Pythagorean ideas in it (Nauta in Marenbon, 2009: 274).

Usener regarded the *Consolation* as a mechanical combination of Aristotle with Neoplatonism, but Rand and Klingner took it to be an original work. Indeed, it set the style for works to follow (Patch, 1935: 4–5). Patch noted that like Plato, Boethius had the mind of a poet with which to take flight, and like Aristotle, a rational conscience for ballast (Patch, 1935: 6).

We can conclude that Boethius exerted a formative influence on medieval culture and life, given his translations from Greek philosophy into Latin and the fact that his books on arithmetic, logic, and music became textbooks for schools where scholars lectured from their content. Education inspired by Boethius particularly flourished in the monasteries established by St. Benedict and others. Also many of the songs in the *Consolation* were set to music, particularly at Oxford and Cambridge.

To console himself after losing Beatrice, Dante apparently set himself the task of reading the *Consolation* because he saw it as written for consolation by a captive and an exile (Stewart, 1891: 92). Dante was strongly influenced by the *Consolation* as is evident in the cosmology of *The Divine Comedy*. Also the fallen angels in Milton's *Paradise Lost* debate the questions of providence, foreknowledge, free will, and fate that are explored in the *Consolation*.

In the sixteenth century, Queen Elizabeth 1st of England is said to have made a swift translation of the *Consolation*. She was fluent in Latin and her translation follows the original faithfully but is not free from errors. There is a view that she turned to the *Consolation* after hearing news that Henry of Navarre had converted to Catholicism in order to become king of France.[15] Although the *Consolation* had been widely translated into many languages, by the nineteenth century, the vision and sense of connection with an eternal world had darkened, and the idea of fruition (perfection in coexistence of the whole within the part) was replaced by the idea of progress as linear succession where the part builds towards perfection. It is in fact a great loss for posterity that Boethius' life was cut short before he could complete his intended project of reconciling differences between Aristotle and Plato, because this could have possessed significance for our time, since a true reconciliation would connect a predominantly spiritual view with a matter-of-fact material world.[16] However, the irony is that in having his life cut short, posterity has the gift of *The Consolation of Philosophy*, which otherwise might not have come into being.

Notes

1 There is a long discussion as to whether Boethius studied in Athens (Proclus' Neoplatonism) or in Alexandria. The majority of scholars opt rather (with P. Courcelle) for Alexandria or both (Cornelia de Vogel). Cf. P. Courcelle, Boece et l'ecole d'Alexandrie. *Melanges de l'Ecole francaise de Rome*, vol. 52, 1935, 185–223; Cornelia J. de Vogel, Boethiana I. *Vivarium*, vol. 9, 1971, 52–61; J. Marenbon, *Boethius*, Oxford: Oxford University Press, 2003, 10–14.

2 This could be an argument that Boethius studied in Alexandria: in this school, especially under Ammonius, since they started with Aristotelian logic. Cf. A.C. Lloyd, Athenian and Alexandrian Neoplatonism. *The Cambridge History of Later Greek and Early Medieval Philosophy*, A.H. Armstrong (ed.). Cambridge: Cambridge University Press, 1967, 319–322.

3 Cf. M. Nussbaum recounts that philosophy heals human diseases produced by false beliefs and its arguments are to the soul what the doctor's remedies are to the body. *The Therapy of Desire: The Theory and Practice in Hellenistic Ethics*. Princeton: Princeton University Press, 1994, 14.

4 8. Cf. Jo-Marie Claassen, *Displaced Persons: The Literature of Exile from Cicero to Boethius*. London: Duckworth, 1999, 244f.

5 Speculative science is stated as divided into three kinds: Physics, Mathematics, and Theology. Boethius, De Trinitate II. H.F. Stewart and E.K. Rand, *The Theological Tractates*. Cambridge, MA: Harvard University Press, 1968, 9.

6 The objective of spiritual exercises is to reach the vision of the whole from the point of view of nature. Cf. Hadot, 1995, 190. An important book here is: Joel Relihan, *The Prisoner's Philosophy: Life and Death in Boethius 'Consolation'*. Notre Dame: University of Notre Dame Press, 2007, 53f.

7 Another antecedent of Boethius' 'Consolatio' was Augustine's 'Soliloquium': inner dialogue with Reason. Cf. Brian Stock, *Augustine's Inner Dialogue: The Philosophical Soliloquy in Late Antiquity*. Cambridge: Cambridge University Press, 2010.

8 Cf. Pierre Hadot, *Inner Citadel: The Meditations of Marcus Aurelius*, translated by M. Chase. Cambridge: Harvard University Press, 1998, 35f.

9 Cf. A fundamental book in Boethian studies is: H. Chadwick, *Boethius: The Consolation of Music, Logic, Theology and Philosophy*. Oxford: Clarendon, 1981.

10 Plato's Natural theology was an attempt to show that nature requires the divine as an ultimate causal explanation. Natural theology therefore seeks to show the continuity between science and religion. Morgan, Michael: 'Plato and Greek Religion'. Richard Kraut, ed., *The Cambridge Companion to Plato*. Cambridge: Cambridge University Press, 1992, 240.

11 Cf. on the topic: J. Marenbon, *Boethius*. Oxford: Oxford University Press, 2003, 154f.

12 Boethius speaks of whether Father, Son, and the desire to reconcile faith with reason. Boethius, *The Theological Tractates*. Loeb Classical Library. London: Heinemann, 1968, 37.

13 It is a characteristic feature of Neoplatonism to read Plato together with Aristotle.

14 In Porphyrium dialogus primus, Migne, Patrologia Latina LX1V 11A, quoted by Victor Watts in Boethius, *The Consolation of Philosophy*. London: Penguin Classics, 1999, xxv. It is important to recognize the Latin term behind the word 'mind'. It can be *mens, ratio, animus, or spiritus*. The English word 'mind' can be interpreted in a number of ways, but even Latin words can include alternative interpretations, so it is important to have a sense for the word's meaning within the context of the sentence.

15 An extremely interesting reception of Boethius' 'Consolatio' is a book by John Kennedy Toole (1937–1969) in *A Confederacy of Dunces*. London: Penguin Classics, 2016.

16 Reconciliation of Plato and Aristotle would, according to the philosopher Rudolf Steiner (1861–1925), combine the artist's approach from spirit and feeling with scientific logic into what is effectively a spiritual science.

References

Armstrong, A.H., editor (1967). *The Cambridge History of Later Greek and Early Medieval Philosophy*. Cambridge: Cambridge University Press.

Barrett, H.M. (1940). *Boethius: Some Aspects of His Times and Work*. Cambridge: Cambridge University Press.

Boethius (1968). *The Theological Tractates*. Loeb Classical Library. London: Heinemann.

Boethius (1999) *The Consolation of Philosophy*. Translated by Victor Watts. London: Penguin Classics.

Chadwick, Henry (1981). *Boethius: The Consolation of Music, Logic, Theology and Philosophy*. Oxford: Clarendon.

Claassen, Jo-Marie (1999). *Displaced Persons: The Literature of Exile from Cicero to Boethius*. London: Duckworth.

Courcelle, P. (1935). Boece et l'ecole d'Alexandrie. *Melanges de l'Ecole francaise de Rome*, vol. 52.

Hadot, Pierre (1995). *Philosophy as a Way of Life*. Malden, MA: Blackwell Publishing.

Hadot, Pierre (1998). *Inner Citadel: The Meditations of Marcus Aurelius*. Translated by M. Chase. Cambridge: Harvard University Press.

Ker, W.P. (1923/1955). *The Dark Ages*. London: Thomas Nelson & Sons.

Kraut, Richard, editor (1992). *The Cambridge Companion to Plato*. Cambridge: Cambridge University Press.

Marenbon, John (2003). *Boethius*. Oxford and New York: Oxford University Press.

Marenbon, John, editor (2009). *The Cambridge Companion to Boethius*. Cambridge: Cambridge University Press.

Nussbaum, M.C. (1994). *The Therapy of Desire: The Theory and Practice in Hellenistic Ethics*. Princeton: Princeton University Press.

Patch, H.R. (1935). *The Tradition of Boethius: A Study of His Importance in Medieval Culture*. New York: Oxford University Press.

Relihan, Joel C. (2007). *The Prisoner's Philosophy: Life and Death in Boethius's Consolation*. Notre Dame: University of Notre Dame Press.

Stewart, H.F. (1891). *Boethius – An Essay*. Edinburgh: Blackwood and Sons.

Stewart, H.F. and Rand, E.K. (1968). *The Theological Tractates*. Cambridge, MA: Harvard University Press.

Stock, Brian (2010). *Augustine's Inner Dialogue: The Philosophical Soliloquy in Late Antiquity*. Cambridge: Cambridge University Press.

Toole, John Kennedy (2016). *A Confederacy of Dunces*. London: Penguin Classics.

Vogel, Cornelia J. de (1971). Boethiana I. *Vivarium*, vol. 9.

3 The *Consolation of Philosophy*

The Consolation is presented in five chapter-length books in a single volume. Its arrangement is rhythmical where the whole volume (five books) comprises 40 sections. The prose in each section of book One is prefaced by a poem, except for the final section (1.VII), which is a single poem. The other sections begin with prose and close with a poem, except for the final section (5.VI), which is just prose. This means that the whole (40 sections) includes 39 poems and 39 philosophical texts.[1] The books One and Five are to be distinguished from books Two to Four. In book One, Boethius' problem is diagnosed and a strategy is devised to deal with it (the problem is conceived in terms of the medical metaphor of *illness and cure*), and book Five considers a fresh topic, closing with a soliloquy, perhaps indicating that the patient has been healed and reduced to contented silence. Books Two to Four are concerned with philosophical arguments where the healing dosage (philosophical argument) is steadily increased. The prayer-poem in book 3, section IX, is a central turning point. This emphasizes the musical (proportional) arrangement of the composition. The circle and sphere (as perfect forms) have symbolic significance within the work. The composition conforms to the established genre of Menippean satire where text alternates with verse.

The dramatic dialogue proceeds with reasoned argument and the poems provide relief from some of the unrelenting logic, or emphasize and endorse the argument, allowing time for reflection. In the course of the dialogue, a wide perspective opens up where the earthly world is seen as subject to the Wheel of Fortune, so that at one time, circumstances are agreeable and in the next moment misfortune reverses the situation. But when the world of time is seen within the perspective of a divine eternity, Boethius discovers that he is able to accept the situation where injustice in the earthly world is not final, and that ultimately divine justice rules and is the final arbiter of fate. Caught like a butterfly in a net, the urgency of Boethius' existential situation creates in him the need to understand the Truth and meaning of

DOI: 10.4324/9781003226093-3

his life. He believes that the human being has resources within to find Truth through contemplation and reason, and accepts Plato's idea that knowledge is 'recollection' (anamnesis). The process of remembering is adopted here where the medicine administered is dialogue with philosophy as wisdom, represented in person by the goddess of philosophy, Philosophia. The discourse and narrative develop slowly, starting with morbid recrimination on the part of Boethius as protagonist, leading on to a conclusion that is able to offer true consolation.

What now follows is a summary to convey the narrative sequence and content in *The Consolation of Philosophy*, with special focus on what is relevant for the guiding question of the oikos. The purpose of this summary is to give a foundation for the application of its ideas to economics.

The text referred to is the translation by Victor Watts, revised in 1999 for *Penguin Classics*, London, 1999, based on Weinberger's text of *Corpus Scriptorum Ecclesiasticorum Latinorum*, LXVII, Vienna/Leipzig, 1934, and the edition of L. Bieler in the *Corpus Christianorum*, *Series Latina* XCIV, Turnhout, 1957.

a. Book I

Boethius was outraged at the injustice of his situation and distressed at his impotence to affect his sentence of imprisonment and execution, since he was not given an opportunity to defend himself. Roman law was respected and authoritative but in this case had been overridden by Theodoric, who feared for his position because of recent political and religious developments. As a consequence, Boethius gives vent to his pain in the opening poem.

1. I

Traumatized and dejected by the downturn in his fortune, the muses of poetry indulge Boethius in his gloomy mood. A woman then appears before him whom he cannot identify. Her appearance is awe-inspiring. At one time, she is of normal height and at another taller than the sky. The self-woven clothes she wears are of 'imperishable material' (suggesting imperishable ideas carefully woven together). The lower hem is embroidered with the Greek letter *Pi* and the top with *Theta* with a ladder connecting them. This arguably indicates the idea of two types of philosophy: *Pi:* practical (moral philosophy and ethics), and *Theta:* the summit of Platonic philosophy (theoria), which is a contemplative view of the highest reality to which philosophy can lead, which includes theology.[2] This image can be seen as representing a relationship between the material and the spiritual–moral within life. The soul (philosophy), as the mid-point on this ladder, mediates between the divine and natural existence; oikos relates to these different levels and unites them. Here, Philosophy is the engine for reflection on the source, the end, and the means, which is seen as the Good. Here, the oikos has its role within the perspective of the meaning of life's journey. It is also interesting to note here that the Greek letter *Theta* was always put on the garments of those sentenced to death,[3] and death provokes motivation for engaging with philosophy. Boethius' visitor is regal in appearance, holding books in her right hand and a sceptre in her left. She imperiously dismisses the muses of poetry that are indulging passion in Boethius. From her perspective as the goddess of philosophy, these muses of poetry are fickle and have no helpful medicine to offer (Boethius, 1999: 3–5).

1. II

This mysterious woman comments in metrical song on Boethius' state of mind. Her offering of poetry in song appears ironic after dismissing the poetic muses, but while the influences of the muses of poetry may be fickle, she, as wisdom personified, is steadfast and rational. Line four of the song specifically states that the mind forgets its inward light. This light is needed for insight. Finishing her song, she reveals her identity as the goddess of philosophy and says it is her intention to restore him to health. She has realized that in his depressed mood, he has temporarily forgotten his true identity. Suddenly, with a fold of her garment, she wipes away his cloud of worldly concern that his tears reveal and refers to the North wind as having the ability to clear dark clouds away (Boethius, 1999: 5–6). A Muse was a spiritual source of inspiration. Poets, such as Homer, invoked the Muse at the beginning of an epic poem and the reality of these godlike beings was taken for granted in ancient times.

Philosophia's garment is torn, which raises the question of *wholeness*, because she says that the rents in her garment are evidence of marauders who tore off parts of the garment thinking they had the whole of philosophy. But of course, a part is only meaningful within the whole. Similarly, Boethius' temporary memory disturbance (through trauma) is the cause of disharmony in his mind as a whole. He needs to be restored to *wholeness* (health) so that his reason can function effectively. Although Philosophia appears as if externally on stage in a drama, the text also resembles an internal dialogue in Boethius' mind. For this reason, *Consolation* has a surreal, dreamlike quality, where the mind is projected partly outwards into the world of appearances and inwards to a world of ideas, where Boethius' soul is the bridge.

1. III

When Philosophia wiped away Boethius' tears, the darkness engulfing him dispersed, enabling his former sight to return and his grief to dissolve. He then regained the ability to be receptive to the light. With his sight restored, he recognized Philosophia as his former nurse and asked the reason for her descent from heaven to be with him in his misfortune. She reassured him of her support and desire to restore him to health, and made the observation that many philosophers had suffered death for the sake of philosophy, because True philosophy angers wicked people. Her list of martyrs included Socrates, whom she said she was with at the time of his victorious death. However, she admitted that when adverse forces are too abundant, the *General* conducts a tactical withdrawal to the *strong point* (the citadel of the soul) (Boethius, 1999: 7–8).

1. IV

Preparing her medicine, Philosophia suggests that men should compose themselves to live at peace in spite of good or bad fortune, and should discard *hope* and *fear* in order to disarm the tyrant's wrath[4] (Boethius, 1999: 8). Boethius had not yet discarded hope and fear but was composing himself ready to jettison these chains. Living strictly in the present can have the effect of achieving freedom in one's soul. It was important that Boethius accepted his situation and that he was fully present. Philosophia asks Boethius if he has understood what she has said, and explain why he is so upset. He takes this as an invitation to indulge his passions, and in his long monologue complains about the injustice done to him. It was philosophy, so he says, that brought him to his condemned fate under tyranny, since he was inspired to enter public service through Plato's ideal set out in the *Republic*, that a commonwealth would be blessed if ruled by philosophers. Activated by a sense of justice, he wanted to counteract the influence of evil people in government, but it was precisely his high moral standards and honesty that contributed to his undoing. By acting justly, he made enemies who, according to him, bore false witness against him (Boethius, 1999: 8–15).

1. V

A long prayer is sung in response to Boethius' gloom. It refers to harmony in the heavens but disharmony in society, and closes with a plea for harmony in the human world by echoing a sentiment in the model Christian prayer known as the Lord's Prayer: 'Thy will be done on earth as it is in heaven'.[5] After listening to Boethius' lengthy account of his grief, Philosophia remains unmoved. She knows of his banishment from his home, but it wasn't until he spoke of it that she realized how far he was banished; he had banished himself by wandering from his *home*. She says that it is the seat of his mind that concerns her and since he is so disturbed, she will commence his treatment by initially applying gentle medicine to his wound (Boethius, 1999: 15–18).

1. VI

Philosophia's prayer concludes with the idea that God does not allow success to any person who steps beyond the natural order of things. She then questions Boethius to comprehend his state of mind: whether life consists merely of chance events, or it is governed by a rational principle. He says he knows that God the creator watches over his creation. She then asks by what means God guides the creation. He says he doesn't know what the question means. Philosophia concludes from this that his mind is still bound by the fever of emotional distraction. In the *Laws*, Plato establishes philosophical theism or 'Natural Theology' as a reasonable demonstration of the being of God.[6] Boethius knows this and even while distressed had not forgotten nature's evidence of a 'Divine Artificer', and yet for him injustice in life and suffering of the innocent seems to deny the just rule of the world.

Philosophia asks Boethius if he *remembers* what is the end and purpose of things and the goal of Nature. He replies that he did once but his memory is affected by grief. Philosophia knows Plato spoke of this and that Boethius also knows it but his knowledge remains clouded. Although Boethius pleads loss of memory, he says that it would be incredibly valuable to have such knowledge if it were True knowledge and not mere speculation. Then, Philosophia asks if he knows what is the source of all things. He says it is God. From this answer, she realizes that grief can disturb the mind and yet not fully overcome it. Then, she asks if he remembers that he is a man. Of course he does, so she asks him what man is. He replies that man is a rational and mortal animal. She asks if he is sure that he is not something more. He replies that he is quite sure. Now she realizes that in his confusion, he has forgotten his *true nature* and this is responsible for his feeling of homelessness and loss. She then knows that her medicine must be directed to restoring his memory. She has hopes of this because he has an inkling that events do not happen by chance but according to divine governance (Boethius, 1999: 18–20).

1. VII

Philosophia sings of light piercing the darkness, and ends with an eloquent expression of the idea that if Boethius wants to follow the path leading to

Truth he should adopt a moderate stance between the extremes of joy and fear, and banish hope and grief (Boethius, 1999: 21).

Aristotle had proposed that man is a rational animal and introduced the idea of the mean between extremes as virtue achieved through balance.[7] Boethius speaks later of philosophy dwelling in him and cleansing him morally, but for practical purposes, his knowledge needs to affect his feelings in order to have its fortifying effect in stability and equanimity. This raises the question of the true nature of knowledge and the contribution of feeling.

b. Book II

2. I

Philosophia fully diagnoses the cause and nature of Boethius' condition: he longs for his former good fortune, yet his imagination holds him in the grip of passion. She reminds him that he used to argue against the flattery of Fortune, so that something has happened to disturb his mind. She then begins her cure with an application of the 'mild and pleasant nourishment' of rhetoric and music. This is music in the form of song. Among the seven liberal arts, music was part of the macrocosmic-heavenly *quadrivium* and rhetoric was part of the microcosmic-earthly *trivium*; so the mediation in this 'medicine' is between the heavenly and the earthly (Boethius, 1999: 22).

Philosophia observes that Fortune's revolving wheel creates constant change and yet Prudence can calculate an outcome. But Boethius has committed himself to the wheel and if it should ever halt it would end its earthly action. He can still be happy, suggests Philosophia, if he knows where his True happiness lies, which is within, so that any loss due to change in fortune should not affect true happiness for this lies in being in control of the Self, and this cannot be taken away from a person. Happiness is therefore understood to be independent from mutable Fortune. Here, Philosophia's song refers to Fortune's impassive stance where, for Fortuna, a person's rise is no more significant than their fall (Boethius, 1999: 23–24). Fortune was once seen as a goddess who moved the circle of the zodiac, but here she is a spirit concerned with the earthly sphere and not a cosmic being of the nature of a goddess.

2. II

Arguing on behalf of Fortuna, Philosophia reminds Boethius that he was born into the world naked,[8] and has prospered, and should appreciate this and realize that favours received from Fortune cannot be claimed as possessions because her benefits are provided as to a person who has use of another's possessions.[9] Fortune can provide wealth but a being endowed with a 'godlike rational nature' should be content with the necessities nature supplies and not seek for material possessions, because 'a mind made in the image of God' needs no adornment. It was God's will, says Philosophia, that man should rule all creatures, but if acquisitions weigh him down, he becomes lower than other creatures, lost in material delusions. A further consequence of material wealth, she says, is that it can bring harm to its owner who becomes a target for criminal activity. It is man's 'insatiable greed' that tries to bind fortune to constancy, but Fortune's essence is inconstancy. Change is part of the order of things but while the heavens are constant, nature is subject to changing cycles. Philosophia then repeats these points in song on behalf of Fortuna (Boethius, 1999: 24–26).

2. III

Philosophia asks Boethius if he has a just defence against Fortune's arguments. He accepts that the rhetoric and music are compelling but says that when these cease then his pain and melancholy return. Philosophia understands this because she has administered only a preliminary poultice to help soothe his grief. She then says that at the right time, she will apply medicine that is calculated to penetrate deep inside. She then reminds him of all the benefits bestowed on him by Fortune and that this is the first time that Fortune has changed toward him, but he has to realize that in any case Fortune deserts a person at the end of life when they die (Boethius, 1999: 27–29).

There is a sense in which Boethius' banishment and death sentence can be seen as gain instead of loss. He was riding high in public esteem with his appointment as Head of the Civil Service and Senate, with both of his sons established as Consuls, so this reversal creates a situation in which he can evaluate his gain and loss in the context of the divine order which transcends the inconstant Wheel of Fortune. For Aristotle, virtue was its own Good, and in the light of this, Boethius has to consider where is his True home, whether in Rome, or philosophy, in his own soul, or in his eternal Heavenly Father's house. Philosophia wanted Boethius to recognize that happiness should be independent of circumstances, because as a mortal able to relate to ultimate Being, he could be assured of the immortality of his soul.

2. IV

Boethius accepts Philosophia's wisdom but complains that to have once been happy and then be deprived of good fortune makes him feel wretched. He is reminded that he is suffering because of his misguided belief, and yet he still enjoys the gifts of Fortune in his family relationships, and a happy person should know where their True happiness lies. Philosophia explains that it is of the nature of human affairs that they cause anxiety because of the incompleteness of prosperity, and Fortune's inconstancy. Escape from Fortune's Wheel lies in its unmoving centre. Philosophia asks why mortal humans seek outside themselves for happiness when it lies within. The 'hinge' for happiness is said to lie in possessing oneself, and Self-possession cannot be taken away by fickle fortune. Boethius is reminded that he was once fully convinced by numerous proofs that the mind survives death and therefore he must accept that True inner happiness endures while Fortune's 'false happiness' ends with death. These thoughts are then echoed in song (Boethius, 1999: 29–33).

2. V

In considering wealth, Philosophia argues that money reveals its value when it is in circulation, and the person who hoards money impoverishes others by disturbing its even distribution. Nature is wealth for everyone, she says, but it cannot be owned, and he who has much wants more, while on the contrary, a person who measures their wealth according to the needs of nature and not ostentation needs least. Material wealth also attracts covetousness and criminality. Philosophia states that a being of 'Godlike rational nature' should glory in this and not in material possessions, for it is the Creator's will that the human race should rule earthly creatures, yet in greed for material things, man degrades himself to a position beneath the lowest of all. Otherwise Man towers above the rest of creation so long as he recognizes his own nature. Indeed to be ignorant of one's likeness to God can be considered a moral defect (Boethius, 1999: 33–37).

2. VI

Philosophia says that having a sense of *power* can be an illusion, as in the case of a wicked person who is in a position of power and yet does not really possess power if they are overcome by lust. Similarly, the virtue of an office does not transfer to the office holder but manifests in the holder's character. Conversely, holding high office can also have the disadvantage of bringing vices to light, as in the case of the emperor Nero. People would laugh, says Philosophia, if they saw a community of mice with one of them exercising power and jurisdiction over the others, and yet there are tyrants in the human community, although a tyrant lives in fear of losing power because power is not a personal possession. While power can be exercised over a person's body and possessions, a mind that is settled in inner tranquillity cannot be moved. Philosophia argues that there is nothing intrinsically good about riches, power, high office, or fame, and that a rich person who is greedy is never satisfied. Riches, power, and status have to be seen in the light of 'inner enrichment', and loss, as in reduction of kingly power, can be a cause of unhappiness (Boethius, 1999: 37–40).

2. VII

In mentioning Fame, Philosophia does not rule out the possibility that Boethius had entered public service to seek fame. She evaluates fame here in terms of the relation between time and eternity: what is the point of fame if the body and soul perish in death? This is the Stoic view from above, beyond the small self. Philosophia then compares the value of earthly fame with the value of possessing spiritual being: if consciousness survives death, she says, it is likely that life afterwards will engage all one's attention so that there will be no room for earthly concerns. Philosophia considers that maintaining a good conscience and exercising virtue are more important than fame, since virtue contributes to the development of perfection and this is where an individual gains the *key* to immortality (Boethius, 1999: 40–44).

2. VIII

Returning to the topic of fortune, Philosophia argues paradoxically that bad fortune is of more value to a man than good fortune, for good fortune deceives while bad fortune enlightens. Additionally, good fortune can lure a person away from the path of 'true good' but bad fortune has the power to draw a person back to their true good. Certainly, Boethius' misfortune revealed to him his true friends. Good fortune can also lead to illusion and enslavement of the mind of the rich in their riches, while bad fortune is like practical teaching from philosophy. She then repeats these ideas in song with sentiments in accordance with the medieval idea of the *Great Chain of Being*, where God is supreme above, binding all interconnected lower levels together through love. Decidedly, sings Philosophia, the rift between the order in nature and disorder in the human world could be healed if love that ruled in nature ruled in human hearts (Boethius, 1999: 44–46).

c. Book III

3. I

After listening to this song, Boethius pleads for Philosophia's 'sharp medicine'. She replies that he would be even more eager for healing if he realized that her medicine would bring him true happiness. But she says that first she will try to sketch an idea of the cause of happiness (Boethius, 1999: 47–48).

3. II

Philosophia says that in seeking happiness, all mortal men in effect seek the good, for the true good, as beatitude, is complete within itself, and needs no addition from outside to complete it. However, some people confuse means with ends, desiring riches for the sake of power and pleasure, but each person in their own way seeks happiness as the supreme Good. Wealth, status, power, fame, and pleasure do relate to happiness and have their value, but according to Philosophia, they are not self-sufficient in themselves (Boethius, 1999: 48–51).

Happiness as beatitude is spoken of as complete: as possession of the Good. This suggests that if the supreme Good can be found and possessed in life, in spite of prevailing circumstances, the end of the journey is attained. The point is that the Good is to be found within; nature holds the reins and all things return to their source for satisfaction, and the circle is complete.

3. III

Philosophia says that people have an instinctive drive towards happiness, which is toward the true good, but error leads a person astray, and if there is something missing after attaining a particular end, then it is spurious. She then asks Boethius if he is fully satisfied with his previous good fortune. He admits that he cannot remember a time when his mind was free from worry. She responds, saying that nature is satisfied with little, but nothing satisfies greed, and riches can create their own sense of incomplete happiness, for material wealth does not represent self-sufficiency, and money does not provide for every need: desire is infinite but the world is finite (Boethius, 1999: 51–53).

3. IV

Philosophia observes (for the second time to reinforce her message) that high office does not bestow virtue on its holder, but on the contrary brings vice to light through exposure to the public gaze, and surely Boethius must have seen the danger when he took office with Decoratus, a thoroughly evil person.[10] Unworthy holders of high office when exposed to public gaze are despised, says Philosophia, for such people degrade the office. High office has no virtue in itself and so has none to bestow on the holder, and on the contrary, virtue in itself transfers worth to those who possess it. All offices are nothing without virtue! (Boethius, 1999: 54–56).

3. V

Philosophia considers kingship and the power it confers but points to an inability to maintain power. She cites the case of Dionysius the Tyrant of Syracuse who portrayed his anxious condition by dangling a sword suspended by a single hair over the head of Damocles. Boethius is assured that power is unstable and is a partial good that can turn into its opposite, while what is complete will not change. The sacredness of friendship is then mentioned: the powerful do not have true friends, she says, and friends of kings can also suffer, as in the case of Seneca when the emperor Nero commanded him to commit suicide. Kingship may command vast swathes of land, but if preyed upon by care and want then even a king is nothing but a slave (Boethius, 1999: 56–58).

3. VI

Philosophia suggests that *fame* is shameful and deceptive, because it results from praise and can be gained by false opinion. If fame is deserved, it cannot influence the philosopher who measures happiness by the voice of conscience. Fame is relative and popularity is subject to chance and change over time, and if nobility derives from fame then it is borrowed nobility. The essential demand on nobility, says Philosophia, is to maintain ancestral standards of virtue, and mankind derives nobility from being the creation of God, but if a person becomes alienated from this source they will tend to cherish meaner things (Boethius, 1999: 58–59).

3. VII

Philosophia speaks of bodily pleasure and concludes that its pursuit is full of anxiety, remorse, and potential for pain and illness, and that excessive indulgence results in sorrow. Although pleasure derived from having a wife and children may be honest, she says, it is never without anxiety and the possibility that children might turn into tormentors. Her song then reinforces the idea that all pleasures have something in common: they drive their devotees with a goad and like bees that offer honey they can return and sting (Boethius, 1999: 59–60).

3. VIII

Philosophia asserts that the five false Goods that she has described cannot satisfy, and they represent misleading side-paths, and are worthless when compared with the vault of heaven and the order ruling there. One's gaze should be directed upward toward one's heavenly origin. She then sings that what men should rightly seek above they seek below on the earth, and this effectively means pursuit of a false path. When this false Good is achieved and its falseness experienced, it is then possible to become aware of the True Good (Boethius, 1999: 60–62).

3. IX

Philosophia affirms that true happiness is self-sufficient, and false happiness is the result of dividing this simple unity into parts. Boethius agrees that true happiness makes a person self-sufficient, strong, worthy of respect, glorious, and joyful, and that these states form a unity that bestows any one of them. Philosophia then affirms that false Goods are mortal and degenerate, and as such are shadows of the Good. She then states that true happiness is a supreme Good, and because Plato prayed for divine inspiration to gain insight, Boethius must agree that she should pray to the 'Father of all things' for guidance to discover the source of the true Good. Her prayer then blends a Platonic hymn, influenced by the *Timaeus*,[11] with Christian prayer, producing a poetic synthesis. This magnificent hymn to the Heavenly Father forms the central turning point in the *Consolation*. The idea that 'soul revolves around the mind' echoes Neoplatonism.[12] God is also seen as the centre of the Ptolomaic planetary system, and the prayer is directed to this source of the Good (Boethius, 1999: 63–67).

This excerpt from the prayer to the Father effectively petitions for the mind to see the source of the Good, the Lord, path and end: the Father who is rest and peace to those who worship.

> Da, pater, augustam menti conscendere sedem,
> Da fontem lustrare boni, da luce reperta
> In te conspicuos animi defigere uisus.
> Dissice terrenae nebulas et pondera molis
> Atque tuo splendore mica; tu namque serenum,
> Tu requies tranquilla piis, te cernere finis,
> Principium, uector, dux, semita, terminus idem.[13] (Boethius, 2014: 85, 10-16).

3. X

Now Boethius comprehends the Form of the 'imperfect' and the 'perfect', so it is time to reveal where perfect happiness is to be found. Applying logic, Philosophia equates supreme happiness with the Good, and supreme Good with God, consequently true happiness is found in God, the origin of all things, and in substance the Supreme Good. Instead of gaining these qualities from outside, God is these things that are Good. Philosophia then concludes her argument with the corollary that supreme happiness is identical with supreme divinity: a happy individual is divine by participation in the divine, but God is divine by nature. Happiness is sought in many ways, she says, but what is strived for essentially in this is the Good. This is said to be the 'hinge' for motivation: the Good or Goodness is what all things aspire to as their end, and because it is agreed that happiness and God are the same, God is found in Goodness (Boethius, 1999: 68–73). The question that Boethius was unable to answer originally about the end and purpose of things and goal of Nature finds its answer here: God is the supreme, all-inclusive Good and aim and end of the whole universe.

3. XI

Philosophia asks how valuable it would be for Boethius to know the Good. He says it will be infinitely valuable if he can also see God who is the Good. She says that she will clarify things using unimpeachable logic, saying that living things exist as a unity but when broken into parts they cease to live; therefore, unity is sought instinctively for the sake of self-preservation, and all things desire unity, which is the same as Goodness; therefore, the end of all things is the Good. After this her song recommends turning one's gaze inward to discover truth, with wandering thoughts circling home (Boethius, 1999: 74–78). This image can be interpreted as meditation where wandering thoughts circle around a central light. This harmonizes with the geocentric image of the cosmos. According to Plato, it is through such meditation that the human being recalls what once he knew and lost.[14]

3. XII

Boethius accepts Plato's doctrine of anamnesis (recovery of forgotten memories) and when Philosophia asks if he can remember how the world is governed, he says that it is ruled by God, because he cannot see what other power could coordinate everything in nature. God rules by force of the Good: transcending but not replacing Fortune's wheel at the helm. Philosophia is now close to helping Boethius acquire true happiness so that he can return safely to his 'true homeland'. She continues to apply logic: God is the Good itself and it is through His goodness that He rules over all things, and since all things incline towards the Good, they are governed in harmony; anything that goes against the Good deviates from its own nature and is no match for the power of the Supreme Good; therefore, God rules over all. This argument satisfies Boethius, and Philosophia introduces a 'conflict of arguments' to ignite sparks of insight. Boethius experiences this as a 'labyrinth of logic' in which he loses his way. Calming himself, he recalls the recent reasoning that led step by step to its conclusion. Philosophia insists that she is not mocking him and that it was the preparatory prayer to God that enabled logic to lead to the realization that the Form of the Divine Substance is identical with the Good, and happiness is self-sufficient. She then sings of the happiness of those who leave the chains of the earth behind to perceive the shining fount of Good. Her song ends with the story of Orpheus who journeyed to Hades to rescue Eurydice: as she was following him on the journey upwards to the surface, he looked back and in doing this, by prior agreement, lost her[15] (Boethius, 1999: 78–84).

If Eurydice is the mind that seeks to rise up to the day, then the message is to not look back when seeking the higher world. Orpheus' weakness was passion, but the secret of virtue is to direct passion towards the Good, to overcome other passions. True happiness is *beatitude*, which includes the complete set of the previously mentioned qualities of the Good. This is to be distinguished from worldly happiness that arises from good luck.

d. Book IV

4. I

Boethius compliments Philosophia on her logic and song, which reassures him but does not address the distress he feels at how, within a world guided by a 'good helmsman', evil can flourish. She advises him that from God's perspective sin never goes unpunished and virtue is rewarded. Fortunately, Philosophia's preliminary arguments had convinced Boethius of the nature of true happiness (as beatitude that combines the five aims strived for), so she is able to proceed and give his 'mind wings' on which to lift itself to return to his 'homeland'.[16] She sings of wings for traversing the heavens to enter the presence of God. This is an imaginative winged journey of the soul through the seven spheres of the Ptolomaic universe to arrive at the Primum Mobile, a point of initiation where all is reversed so that the periphery becomes the centre, from where the 'Unmoved Mover' turns the chariot of the universe. Philosophia says that this journey will allow him to remember his home and his source and end (Boethius, 1999: 85–87).

4. II

Boethius' desire is kindled to return to his true homeland, but Philosophia warns that for anything to be achieved a person needs 'will' and 'power'. She reminds him that since everyone seeks happiness, which is a Good, both good men and bad men seek the Good because of the natural inclination towards the Good, and men become Good by acquiring Goodness, and the good obtain this by exercising virtue, but the evil person fails by following personal desires. This failure reveals a lack of power, while the cause of departure from virtue to vice is either ignorance or the lure of pleasure. In either case, this is weakness. Philosophia says that men who deliberately choose vice ultimately cease to be, because in going against their own nature, they cannot preserve their existence. Realizing the Good is Self-realization, and since we are moral beings, this includes attainment of morality. A power that can only do Good is omnipotent, but human beings that can do evil are not powerful in this way. Philosophia agrees with Plato in his *Gorgias* that only the wise can achieve their desire while the wicked are busy with pleasure and so miss their real objective.[17] Even a powerful king, Philosophia says, can become a slave if his will is deposed by greed (Boethius, 1999: 87–92).

4. III

Philosophia insists that goodness is its own reward. Goodness is happiness, and happiness is divine so that the good person is a god. This achievement of goodness means alignment of one's true human nature with the divine nature, and constitutes participation in the divine; true happiness is recognition of one's inner divinity; goodness is rewarded and wickedness is punished. Wickedness thrusts a person down below the human so that human nature is lost. A wicked person cannot rise to the divine so sinks to the level of an animal: man's true self is dethroned and the mind becomes like that of an animal. Philosophia identifies three means of error: ignorance, lack of self-control, and knowingly and willingly doing wrong. Each of these goes against human nature, causing a person to lose connection with their 'essence'; for in going against God, a person cannot preserve their own nature. Philosophia stresses in her song that the human is poised between the divine and the animal, and she refers to Circe's enchantment that affected the homeward-bound companions of Odysseus who were turned into animals, but restored by the winged god Hermes.[18] Philosophia intimates that Circe's enchanted draught changed the body but not the inner person. However, she makes the point that there are poisons that can 'dethrone a man's true self' (Boethius, 1999: 93–96).

4. IV

When Boethius accepts that wicked people retain their human body while their minds can revert to the animal level, Philosophia insists that wicked people are miserable, but death ends this, for if life extended endlessly the misery would be everlasting for an immortal soul. She says if her conclusions are difficult to accept then the assumptions on which they are based should be examined. Then, based on the premise that punishment as a means of justice is good, she argues that punishment alleviates unhappiness because the wicked are happier when they are punished. There is cleansing punishment after death, says Philosophia, but that is not her point. It is because of Boethius' concern for wickedness seeming to go unpunished that she offers her explanation: although the wicked might seem powerful they have no 'real' power. She then says that in the order of creation people choose either to look up to higher things or to gaze downward, and the direction of their gaze is their own responsibility. Additionally, those who commit injustices are more miserable than those who suffer them, and criminals should be treated with sympathy for their illness of abandoning virtue, because this is a disease of the mind. A healthy mind is produced from goodness, and illness is the result of wickedness. Philosophia then sings of injustice where men might prey upon wild animals but should not be the prey of other men. Her song concludes on the positive note that there is no just cause for aggression; men should love the Good and pity the bad (Boethius, 1999: 96–101).

4. V

Boethius remarks that it is hard to distinguish between chance and an intervention of God when the good often suffer and the wicked prosper. Philosophia explains that ignorance of the divine plan need not prevent the belief that a Good power rules the universe and that what happens is ultimately right. Her song then refers to movements in the celestial heavens where the constellation of the Great Bear (Arcturus) revolves around the hinge of the Unmoved Mover. This is intended to illustrate that if a person knows exactly how this whole system functions, then it would not be a mystery, since it is hidden causes that evoke perplexity (Boethius, 1999: 101–103).

4. VI

Boethius begs to understand the hidden causes of injustice in life: why good men receive punishment suitable to crime, while bad men can receive rewards suited to virtue. Philosophia says that everything is ordered from the unity of the mind of God, and when the order of the plan is seen from God's point of view this is called Providence, but otherwise is known as Fate. Providence is divine reason and Fate is the order of things subject to change. When seen with God's foresight, this plan is Providence, and the same unified whole when unfolded in the course of time is Fate. They are different but one depends on the other. Here, Philosophia uses the geometric analogy of a point with concentric circles around it: the circular orbits close to the centre are nearer to the perfection of Providence while those further away are more subject to Fate in their longer journey through time. The interrelationship here is between the winding course of Fate and the direct simplicity of Providence: between reasoning and understanding, coming into being and eternity, and between the moving circle and the still central point (Boethius, 1999: 103–105).

Philosophia explains that it is because men cannot contemplate the 'order of events' from the divine perspective that things in life seem so confused. Providence, she says, stings some people to avoid giving happiness for too long, while allowing others to be vexed by 'hard fortune' to strengthen their 'virtues of mind', and encourage the exercise of patience. She says that God directs all towards Goodness by means of the chain of necessity presided over by Fate. Then to relieve Boethius' confusion, she sings to assure him that if he wishes to understand the laws of God he must observe the overall harmony of the heavens, and perceive its relationship to earthly affairs. It is, she says, out of love that God corrects any wandering from the true path so that by the response of love there is return to recognition of God as the source of all things. She says that Love holds all together, and participation in the eternal depends on the fire of attention to the Good (Boethius, 1999: 106–111).

4. VII

Philosophia insists that all fortune is good, either as reward or as punishment to correct the bad. Boethius finds this difficult to comprehend but is finally persuaded that a wise man can learn from adverse fortune, and this is where virtue is valuable for it endures adversity and is not influenced by good or ill fortune; it chooses the balanced path between extremes. It rests with Boethius to make of Fortune what he will. The power of will is emphasized in Philosophia's song in which the 12 labours of Hercules serve to demonstrate the goodness of Fortune, where victory (the activation of virtue) in the trials of Hercules earns him a place in heaven. This is a timely insight for Boethius (Boethius, 1999: 111–115).

e. Book V

5. I

Boethius asks if there is such a thing as chance. Philosophia replies that there has to be a 'cause' because nothing comes out of nothing. If anything happens other than intended then this can be considered chance, but it is actually the result of coincident causes under the rule of Providence. Philosophia quotes Aristotle as saying that whenever something is done for some purpose, and for certain reasons something other than what was intended happens, it is called chance. So what appears to be chance really happens according to the rule of law (Boethius, 1999: 116–118).

5. II

Boethius asks if there is freedom of will within unfolding Fate. Philosophia replies that a creature with reason can make judgements of choice, but it takes will to take advantage of this freedom. Freedom, she says, is the power of judgement: divine beings possess clear-sighted judgement and uncorrupted will to effect their desire, but human souls are more free when contemplating the Mind of God and less free when imprisoned in flesh and blood, and even less free when given over to wickedness, which results in loss of their proper reason. She says that the 'eye of Providence', which from eternity sees the past, present, and future, arranges 'predestined' rewards according to merit (Boethius, 1999: 118–119).

5. III

Boethius asks Philosophia to explain how free will is possible if God has foreknowledge. She explains that events must happen but foreknowledge does not impose necessity on them. She accepts that this is hard to comprehend because human reason cannot approach the 'immediacy' of divine foreknowledge, which does not impose predestination on the future and neither does it impose it on the will. This can be understood when the difference between vision in the world of time is compared with the view from eternity, where everything is complete (Boethius, 1999: 119–123).

5. IV

Philosophia affirms that foreknowledge does not impose predestination on the future, so that the will is still free, and neither does it impose necessity on actions. She says that all that is known depends on the ability to know, for example, through sense perception, imagination, reason, or intelligence, but a more exalted eye of intelligence, with the pure vision of the mind, will comprehend the simple 'form' itself. This superior mode of intuitive knowledge includes the inferior (lower levels), but the inferior vision cannot rise upward to perceive at the level of the superior vision. The human being has particular faculties of knowledge but the vital factor, from Philosophia's perspective, is possession of an active mind that blends images received from outside with forms resident within (Boethius, 1999: 124–129).

5. V

Philosophia says that reason belongs only to the human race, and is a higher faculty of knowledge than sense perception, just as 'intelligence' that applies to 'divinity' is higher than reason. She says that a multiplicity of kinds of knowledge has been given to different substances.[19] She insists that while the higher has knowledge of the lower levels it is not possible for a lower faculty of knowledge to know above and beyond its own level. However, if human reason could raise itself to the cognition of the immediacy of divine intelligence, there would be no difficulty regarding free will, since all would be seen within the union of necessity (Boethius, 1999: 130–132).

5. VI

Continuing her argument, Philosophia says that it is generally agreed that God is eternal, and eternity involves complete, simultaneous, and perfect possession of everlasting life. In contrast, beings existing in time are limited by their participation in the progressive state of becoming. What they lack is the viewpoint that possesses simultaneously the whole fullness of life. The mind of God embraces the whole of everlasting life in one simultaneous present, and the infinite changing of things in time imitates the presence of unchanging life (Boethius, 1999: 132).

Philosophia says that every object of knowledge depends not on its own nature or identity but on the nature of those who comprehend it. She then suggests examination of the nature of the divine substance to see what can be known about its mode of knowledge. She says that those philosophers were mistaken who said that Plato believed the world had no beginning in time and would have no end, in order to maintain that the world is co-eternal with the Creator. She insists that the condition of God is 'eternal presence' and 'omniscience' that transcends time and sees the past, present and future in the immediacy of the present. This is best called Providence or 'looking forth' instead of 'seeing beforehand'. Divine foreknowledge does not change anything; it is seeing all things in an eternal present, just as seeing in the present within the world of time does not alter anything except that it is possible to distinguish between what is willed and what happens of necessity. For divine foreknowledge, future activities appear necessary, but from an earthly perspective, future activities appear to be free. God is omniscient not because the future is known, but because of his 'immediacy'. The power of this knowledge, which embraces all things in present comprehension, has also established the mode of being for all things, and owes nothing to anything secondary to itself. God is able to dispense justice from on high, and free will is uncompromised. Philosophia then asserts that hope placed in God is not in vain, and prayer is still effective if the prayer is of the right kind, and additionally it is better to cultivate virtue and avoid vice and lift the mind up to the right kind of hope. She says that a great necessity is laid upon Boethius to be good if he is to be honest with himself, since he lives in the sight of a judge who sees all things. This is an admonition to live in such a way that it is possible to *realize* human nature and be happy, which in turn activates one's divinity. To be Good is to be happy in union with God as the Form of the Good. This is said to be the end and constitutes the true home of the human being (Boethius, 1999: 133–137).

Notes

1 The number 40 signifies the completion of a process in time: 40 days of the Flood in the days of Noah, and 40 days spent in the wilderness by Jesus before assuming His divine mission.
2 Cf. Boethius, De Trinitate II. *Theological Tractates*. London: Heinemann, 1968, 9 f. Additionally Joseph Milne says these three levels (religious, philosophical, and empirical) are not merely three types of representation, but distinct modes of orientation towards reality, or kinds of engagement with the cosmos. Joseph Milne, *Metaphysics and the Cosmic Order*. London: Temenos Academy, 2006, 19.
3 Cf. H. Chadwick, Theta on Philosophy's Dress in Boethius. *Medium Aevum 49/2*. Oxford: Blackwell, 1980, 175–179.
4 These are the fundamental emotions that prevent us from gaining peace of mind and *autarkeia*. Epicureans and Stoics fought with those emotions (cf. M. C. Nussbaum, *The Therapy of Desire*. Princeton: Princeton University Press, 1994, 83–89, 91–94, 192–238).
5 The *Gospel According to Matthew*, 6:10.
6 This comprises Plato's *Laws* book Ten.
7 According to Aristotle, virtue is concerned with feelings and action, where too much or too little is wrong while the mean between them is right. So virtue is an aptitude for aiming at the mean: Aristotle, the *Nicomachean Ethics*. New York: Oxford University Press, 2009m 1106b.
8 Cf. Book of Job 1, 20–21.
9 The important emphasis here is on the difference between goods that belong to us and those that are not ours. This is a clear reference to Stoicism (Epictetus, *The Discourses of Epictetus: With the Encheiridion and Fragments*. London: Bell, 1912, 1).
10 Decoratus was a young Roman advocate appointed as 'quaestor' in 508.
11 It is stated in Plato, *Timaeus,* 27c that everyone with the least sense always calls on God at the beginning of any undertaking, small or great. Written in hexameter, this is the turning point in *Consolation*. It appears that now the prisoner

takes the initiative and refuses to follow the path of Platonic transcendence; he poses the questions about human freedom and responsibility.

12 Plotinus speaks of the dance of the imperfect around the perfect.

13 Cf. John 14:6. 'Jesus replied, "I am the way; I am the truth and I am life; no one comes to the Father except through me".'

14 Plato, *Phaedo,* 72e. 'Besides Socrates', rejoined Cebes, 'there is that theory which you have often mentioned to us – that what we call learning is really just recollection'.

15 Ovid, *Metamorphoses*. Lincoln: University of Nebraska Press, X–XI.

16 This is a famous motif from Plato's *Phaedrus,* 246b–247a.

17 Plato, *Gorgias*, 466b–481b.

18 Homer, *The Odyssey*, Book 10.

19 Substance is meant here in the Aristotelian sense: the essential nature of a being.

References

Aristotle (2009). *The Nicomachean Ethics*. New York: Oxford University Press.

Boethius (1999). *The Consolation of Philosophy*. Translated by Victor Watts. London: Penguin Classics.

Boethius (2014). *Consolatio Philosophiae*. Edited by Peter Snipes. Open Source Classics. Chicago: Pluteo Pleno.

Chadwick, H. (1980). Theta on Philosophy's Dress in Boethius. *Medium Aevum 49/2*. Oxford: Blackwell.

Epictetus (1912). *The Discourses of Epictetus: With the Encheiridion and Fragments*. London: Bell.

Homer (1988). *The Odyssey*. Edited by H. Bloom. New York: Chelsea House.

Milne, Joseph (2006). *Metaphysics and the Cosmic Order*. London: Temenos Academy.

Nussbaum, M.C. (1994). *The Therapy of Desire: The Theory and Practice in Hellenistic Ethics*. Princeton: Princeton University Press.

Ovid (1970). *Metamorphosis*. Lincoln: University of Nebraska Press.

Stewart, H.F. and Rand, E.K. (1968). *The Theological Tractates*. Cambridge, MA: Harvard University Press.

4 Consolation as Economy's Foundation

What is the economy of philosophy's consolation and how does it differ from mainstream economics? *Consolation* presents an economy with the following alternative attributes: wealth as inner happiness derived from virtues in contrast to inner poverty from hoarding outer possessions; self-sufficiency through recollection of the Whole in opposition to infinite desire for base pleasures; development as fruition from the Good instead of progress defined as infinite growth; the Good as transcendental practice rather than exchange value; and Truth as philosophy's consolation in place of market calculation. *Consolation*'s economy is dynamic yet harmonious, self-sufficient yet recollecting, and logical yet mysterious. Oikos as soul is the dynamic bridge in its circling home and so the economy is the circling home towards virtues. This involves differing levels of dynamic movement around a still centre. Such a foundation is dynamic and open to judgment; it is not static or dogmatic. This is the economy of the love of wisdom and its consolation. Wisdom inheres in the self-sufficiency of the economy and love binds and interconnects the whole.

Philosophy's *Consolation* presents an economy in part governed by the Wheel of Fortune, yet ultimately ruled by Providence. Fate is the necessary unfolding of Providence in time, so *Fate* (as Providence) governs oikos, in contrast to modern economics, where human egoism, shown in self-interest and utility maximization, governs under *Fortuna*. Fortunes can be made and lost in the competitive and unstable modern economy, but the oikos is determined by foresight and the stability of self-sufficiency. Economic thinking from the oikos therefore starts by considering earthly support to enable participation in the Good that enables the *Human* to flourish. The oikos is that aspect of the soul where balance is created and decided, and obtained under the control of reason: hence oiko-nomia, or 'economic reasoning'. So oikos is something like 'balanced soul', or the soul that has achieved a state of balance. In theory, soul can be unbalanced, but the balanced soul is the outcome of a balancing process that is willed.

DOI: 10.4324/9781003226093-4

The *Consolation*'s starting point for economic thinking is the human being, so it is human-centred, where the soul is seen to exist as part of a greater whole. For Boethius wealth means inner richness, and its cultivation is considered vital in a society designed to pursue the Good. Yet fatefully, Boethius found himself as a prisoner, condemned to death because of his pursuit of the Good. The only consideration that impelled him to any high office, so he said, was a general desire for the Good. Boethius' economics teaches that a truly rich person is someone who wants nothing more. The Stoic response to infinite desire was to limit wants to the ready supply available, but a hedonist response was to increase market supply to meet the increasing demand from infinite wants. Today in the light of limits to global supply, it is vital to distinguish basic human *needs* from *wants*. In this respect, the oikos, as household management, presents the case for an economy concerned primarily with the provision of basic needs.

Basic needs include food, shelter, clothing, work, and security. Addressing the issue of basic needs, Manfred Max-Neef's 'Matrix of Needs and Satisfiers'[1] provides a comprehensive list of needs and their means of satisfaction. This includes nine categories of need within four states of existence: Being; Having; Doing; Interacting. The nine categories are Subsistence; Protection; Affection; Understanding; Participation; Idleness; Creation; Identity; Freedom. Additionally, the United Nations Development Group has goals for global development to address basic needs as human rights in their policy of economic transformation to end extreme poverty. On the other hand, the assumption of neoclassical economics is that the individual, as an economic agent, is motivated by the sole aim of maximizing utility above all other considerations, and acts accordingly, and that the principle of maximization of profits applies to *every* business. Yet this narrow utilitarian approach overlooks needs that apply in the broader picture of the individual in society. Here, identifiable bio-cultural needs apply, such as human rights, job security, mental health, literacy, a benign socio-ecological environment, and access to affordable public utilities.

The economy of *Consolation* intentionally limits itself to the satisfaction of basic human needs to enable it to focus on the transcendental purpose of Truth-seeking, and participation in the Good. Indeed, knowledge of the Good[2] is linked to the quest for Truth, and Truth-seeking is linked to 'wealth inside' (C 3m11.1–3). This is at variance with modern neoliberal economics, which roots Truth and wealth in the Market and not in the Human. According to Philip Mirowski, the epistemology of neoliberalism views the market as a great information processor that is superior to any human being, and consequently as the arbiter of Truth.[3] But this 'truth' is the result of abstract calculation in authoritarian market designs, which may produce 'efficient' market outcomes, but diverts attention from the kind of Truth that is rooted in the Human as the fount of oikonomia. Absolute or transcendental Truth concerns the meaning and purpose of life in the context of the cosmos and eternity. *Consolation* speaks of an Eternal Law beyond and within Nature that governs by participation in the whole, in which the part participates through union with the Good. Boethius tells us that for him, Truth would be to meet God.

We must ask ourselves if Truth is found in the external world of facts and figures, like a formula. If it is it will then be truth *relative* to its process of assessment, but essential (objective) Truth has a spiritual dimension: it relates to Being, with which Knowledge is closely linked (if not identical), yielding the possibility of knowing the Truth. The Greek word for Truth: 'aletheia', includes the noun 'lethe', which invokes forgetting and sleep. Truth cannot be totally lost in forgetfulness for arguably it is consciousness itself. Plato's doctrine of anamnesis is concerned with recovery of the memory of who we are and what we know through all eternity. This is the kind of knowledge sought in the admonition: 'know yourself'. This means that the economy of soul, as oikos, is the seat of Truth, which concerns Self-knowledge as recollection (and wisdom through philosophy and poetry), in contrast to a calculus of pleasure and pain, or the exchange values of modern economics. This conception of Truth links to the self-sufficiency of oikos, or the completeness of the Good. A living relationship to knowledge depends upon a person's ability or faculty to know. For the philosopher, John Macmurray, knowledge of the real was not its description but its apprehension, and in that strict sense, science is not knowledge (Macmurray: *Reason and Emotion*, 113). Indeed, the impersonality of the science of modern economics (which ideally should serve the ends of the personal and the concrete) needs to be engaged with values that relate it to reality.[4] This is where the oikos as soul has a living role in mediating between the divine and the earthly.

Aristotle distinguished between two forms of economy: *oikonomia* and *chrematistics*. *Oikonomia* is the management of real resources to supply the necessities of life, and *chrematistics* is the study of material wealth creation. *Consolation* is essentially concerned with oikonomia or oikos as the household economy based on use values,[5] and modern economics is primarily concerned with chrematistics and exchange values. Indeed, now that awareness is growing that the abstract nature of modern economics is instrumental in environmental and social destruction, the ideas discussed by Boethius become livingly relevant in finding an alternative foundation for the economy.

Consolation's oikos reflects ancient culture when the economy was primarily based on agriculture, particularly in classical Greece and Rome where the economy of the household was central with agriculture playing an important role. A land-based oikos was also a feature of medieval Christendom with its reliance on agriculture as the substance of the economy. Historical change during the eighteenth century found reflection in Adam Smith's *Wealth of Nations*, published in 1776. This charted the rising dominance of a market 'exchange' economy over the customary 'use' economy.

Broadly speaking, the medieval economy in Europe was based on the principle of physiocracy. This is the idea that the material wealth of nations derives essentially from the value of land as agriculture, or land development, complemented by productive work. Ideologically the economy was based on biblical principles, an important one being reciprocity: 'do to others what you would have them do to you'. Canon Law was Statute Law for the whole of Christendom so that ethics was included in law. Two important laws affecting economics were *fair price* and *usury*.[6] A fair price was set for the necessities of life relative to the cost of materials, such that the price of bread was related to the market price of corn, and profit through charging interest (usury) was forbidden because this was considered to be making money from money. These principles upheld fairness and the Christian ethic to love your neighbour as yourself, and to respect the human individual made in the image of God. These Christian values were supported by Aristotelian logic in the work of Thomas Aquinas. Indeed it was through the *Consolation*, which was widely read and translated, that Boethius extended into the Middle Ages his potent synthesis of Christian, classical, rational and mystical ideas, which fuse Plato's ideas of the Good with Aristotle's logic and the mysticism of the 'One', associated with Plotinus.

The medieval feudal system exemplifies the use of land as a predominant source of material wealth, where land owned by a local lord was leased to farmers who thereby became obligated to the lord. Monasteries also owned land so that agriculture was the basis of their self-sufficiency.[7] Wealth in the Middle Ages was therefore twofold: it was a product of cooperation between the spiritual and the material, between virtue and land, considered in the context of the soul's relationship to God. This ethical economy, based largely on the resource of land, was supplemented with working trades and markets. The strong sense of community that this arrangement engendered encouraged moral behaviour and a 'for use' economy based on sustainable agriculture. The ideals within this system commend themselves to us today under very different circumstances.

a. Human Being: Between Higher Nature and Basic Needs

Being Towards Death

Boethius was dejected by his sentence of death. This is how the *Consolation* begins, but Philosophia's consoling ideas steadily open up an awareness that goes beyond anxiety about mortality. Philosophia had said that fame is nothing if the soul and body die, because such a person would no longer exist, but if the mind remains conscious after death, then from the vantage point of heaven, earthly things will fade into insignificance (C 2.7.73–78). Indeed, 'remembering' through a forerunning to death brings out the Truth by opening to Being. This Truth is wisdom based on the art of poetic and philosophic understanding as means for embodied spiritual knowledge.

Looking in retrospect to early Greek philosophy, Martin Heidegger spoke of 'Dasein': the being that is there in its world and for whom Being is a question, and where the prospect of death cannot be avoided. Certainly an awareness of mortality raises the question of one's attitude to death: of the relevance of the question of whether there is an eternal state or if death is a complete cessation of personal existence. This question affects an understanding of Being and how life is to be lived, and what economy is suitable for this life. From his twentieth-century standpoint, Heidegger claimed that mortals cannot engage in *dwelling* without the divinities, and dwelling requires a kind of thinking that has, for the most part, been marginalized or even excluded in our technological age, because it presupposes attunement to, and recognition of, immanent divinity.[8] The economy of *Consolation* confronts this need for 'dwelling', because with the soul as oikos, it is the circling home to the centre, to immanent divinity.

Eternity can be an infinite heavenly state (or its reverse), or eternal life can be understood as rhythms of embodiment and disembodiment as reincarnation of an evolving individuality. In these circumstances, the oikos provides earthly support for life that acknowledges its eternal (spiritual) context. If death is understood as the complete end of an individual, then this could encourage an inclination towards maximization of pleasure in an assumed single lifetime. In this light, it is possible for an economy to be seen from an egocentric point of view where natural resources are exploited in the interests of satisfying desires and wants. However, if this is the case, the modern neoclassical economy, as an infinite closed circular flow of goods, services, and money, neglects mortality by assuming continual earthly existence. It ignores the cyclic organic-principle within the finite earthly world, which requires the cycle of organic growth, sustainability, and death. The interrelationship between the finite and the infinite is a key awareness for human life and its economy, and while the neoclassical economy caters for unrestricted greed in a life where death is potentially the end, the oikos takes account of the eternal as the *whole* that transcends (yet embraces) time. Taking account of the whole (eternity) is important because it provides the context that gives meaning to the Good and reason to pursue it on the assumption that physical death is not the end of one's life, and goodness bears fruit. The oikos is therefore concerned with reconciling the earthly and the transcendental.

Death raises the question of identity and inheritance, and extending one's identity by making a will to leave accumulated worldly riches to family members. However, a more just distribution regarding the Whole would be to return this lifetime's accumulation to the *commons* from where it has largely been derived. Indeed, the very notion of survival after death could have the effect of changing a person's priorities, so that more attention is focused on life's purpose, and to the care of the soul in developing 'treasure within', which the basic oikos supports. Fortune plays a significant role in life but within the economy Fortune's role is limited to the earthly finite realm; fore-thinking to death as a source of wisdom reveals Fortune to be an incomplete foundation. Fortune's constant inconstancy as a form of immortality is said to lack Being, while mortals are more connected to Being. Bad fortune can in fact be a teacher. Philosophia speaks of the enlightening potential of bad fortune where the 'good fortune' of riches can enslave the mind while on the contrary 'bad fortune' can have a liberating effect by revealing the fragility of happiness (C 2.8.10–13). As Philosophia says, when one's life is at an end, there is a kind of death for Fortune (C 2.3.p28.26–27).

Basic Needs and Higher Nature

Ancient philosophy aimed to establish a rightful human relationship to reality, and accordingly Boethius relates the human soul to Divinity. Man may be a rational animal, but the essential difference from an animal is that the human has a spirit, which includes reason and a moral sense. Aristotle defined the function of Man as a kind of life that is an activity of the soul or course of action that conforms with reason; so if a good person performs goodness excellently then the good of man is an activity of the soul in accordance with virtue (Aristotle, 2009: 12, 1098a).

Philosophia asks Boethius if he knows 'what a human being is'. This question is asked with the understanding that connecting to life's source relates to wholeness (health). It cannot be under-estimated how important this question is for economics, in relation to whether the human being is made for the economy or whether the economy is made for the human being. Philosophia knows that a person is more than a rational and moral animal, and that in describing creation, Plato had said that the demiurge put intelligence in soul, and soul in body (Plato: *Timaeus* 30a). Here, intelligence is divine spirit. Unfortunately, this combination results in immense conflict. With regard to the trinity of the human being, in the *Timaeus*, Plato speaks of Nous (mind), Psyche (soul), and Soma (body), where nous is the noblest part of the soul. In the *Republic*, he then divides the soul into three: *Logos* (head), *Thymos* (chest), and *Eros* (stomach). Here, Logos is the thinking part of the soul. He then relates these three aspects of the soul to a person and to the government of society: *Logistikon* is a gentle rule through love of learning; *Thymoeides* obeys instructions from *Logistikon* and defends the whole; while *Epithymetikon* seeks and consumes pleasure.[9] When *Logistikon* rules the whole, there is harmony. This is the harmony of *Consolation's* oikos.

From a Platonic perspective, the soul, bearing the spirit, is the individuality that survives death to be reborn at a later time, and so the oikos applies to the body-soul-spirit whole, with emphasis on spirit–soul, because this is essentially the human. It is because of the 'embodiment' of the spirit in the soul that this trinity of body, soul, and spirit is often assumed to be a duality of body and soul. However, the spirit (higher intellect) is vital, since it is the human connection with the divine.[10] When *Consolation* speaks of 'mind', it refers to spirit that is linked to 'intelligence' (the divine intellect).

While Boethius accepted the idea of the embodiment of a spiritual-rational element in man, as a Christian in Rome, he would have also been familiar with the biblical conception (he is known to have written pamphlets defending the orthodox Roman Catholic religion – *De fide catholica*). Biblical and Platonic conceptions have many essential points in common, among them the similar idea that the Lord God formed man from the dust of the earth and breathed into his nostrils the breath of life so that man became a living soul (Genesis 2:7).

Human nature is a combination of the rational mind and the instinctive desire of the animal body. The spirit (mind) within the soul strives 'upwards' while the animal strives earthwards,[11] and the mediation of virtue propels the rational spirit towards the authentic Good. This is where the link with the authentic economy of *Consolation* applies: it is a 'use' economy where goods become useful in pursuing the Good, and economic activity beyond this is not encouraged if it is likely to cause distraction from truth-seeking, offering a false path to happiness. The human body is the means of engagement between the soul-spirit and the earthly world, and the dignity of the body deserves respect in its relationship within the trinity of body-soul-spirit. *Consolation* speaks of the intermediary role of the soul:

> You bridge the parts to the whole by a soul of threefold nature that harmoniously moves all.
>
> (C 3.m9.13–14)

> Tu triplicis mediam naturae cuncta mouentem
> Conectens animam per consona membra resoluis; (Boethius, 2014: 85, 1-2)

From his Platonic stance, Proclus also describes the function of the soul as a bridge. Here, soul, or psyche, is the living psychological entity that interrelates with the spirit (mind) and the body.[12] When Philosophia refers to the 'seat of the mind', she reveals concern for Boethius' soul, which hosts the spirit as the intellectual faculty of reason and knowledge.

This suggests that the wealth of oikos lies in the divine nature of transcendental virtues and is not merely earthly. As home for the soul and as the foundation for inner wealth, the oikos is a basic need economy in which the *nature of the human being* is decisive. Therefore, as an economy, the oikos nourishes the seed of the spirit, enabling it to develop and blossom into language, culture, religion, social relationships, and community.

Glorying in one's spiritual godlike nature does not preclude enjoyment of things,[13] but will exclude glorying in consumerism with its potential to absorb all of one's attention. In this sense, the economy of *Consolation* is an inversion of an economy based on infinite growth where consumption, profiteering, and greed develop the potential to force a person into material and spiritual destitution. By contrast, the oikos of *Consolation* celebrates the Good. Naturally the economy of 'consolation' will meet needs such as housing, physical nourishment, clothing, education and security, but it will do so by distinguishing *needs* from *wants* that might divert attention from participation in the Good. Material poverty, as distinguished from destitution, enables full concentration on the object of one's concern. For example, Jesuits taking the vow of poverty, chastity, and obedience are liberated to pursue their vocation free from material distraction. But poverty as destitution, as in the contemporary crisis of homelessness, is due to the insufficiency of the modern economy in comparison with self-sufficiency of the oikos.

The Good

In *Consolation*, Boethius is incrementally reminded that his spiritual home is in God, and self-sufficiency 'within' takes precedence over outer circumstances. God is the Good, and the Soul is the dwelling place, or oikos (home) of the Human. The economy that arises from this is therefore directed toward social provisioning for basic needs in accordance with the Good to support True well-being.

Possession of the Good is completion, and is the root of self-sufficiency in relation to Being. People become good by acquiring goodness (C 4.3.37), which is the application of virtue that has its own reward in happiness and self-sufficiency. In this way, the self-sufficient oikos is its own reward. The gaze inwards perceives the Self as Truth, which is the Good (the soul has access to everything). What is in common here is the substance, which is self-sufficient. 'Substance' is seen here in Aristotle's sense of a real thing identified by its Form. The Good is the self-sufficient Whole, so possession of the Good connects with Being (as the whole), and brings the eternal (timeless) aspect of the virtues (related to perfection) down to earth into the temporal, finite, and imperfect world. These virtuous foundations of *Consolation*'s oikos differ radically from modern economics, which knows neither death nor the finite, because its motivation is towards infinite growth and an endless flow of goods and money. What modern economics overlooks, with its reductionism and mechanistic understanding of time, is the immanence of the transcendental.

In *Consolation's* central majestic prayer, the soul circling the mind (C 3.m9.16) is said to be in pattern like the World Soul moving the firmament. Indeed, the axle of the Wheel of Fortune is Providence, so the Divine Mind is the centre around which the soul revolves. Similar ideas are found in the Enneads of Plotinus, where the soul is said to circle around the Divine Mind (Plotinus, 1956: Ennead 2.1), and we bear ourselves aloft by that 'intact part' where our centre holds to the centre of all centres, just as the centres of all circles of a sphere coincide with the sphere to which all belong (Plotinus, 1948: 218).

The circle is a key image in the *Consolation*. The Wheel of Fortune traces its circle with its ups and downs, but set against this is the constancy of the heavens revealed in the providential geocentric circles of the planets that wheel around the central earth. Given the wings of Imagination, Boethius can fly from the Earth through the concentric circles of the planets to the outermost boundary. We are told that there an inversion occurs that transforms the geocentric universe into a theocentric one. The human mind (made in the image of God) connects with this centre (God) around which the soul circles (C 3.m9.15–16). For Plotinus the Soul that circles the Divine Mind has its light and image inseparably attached to it (Plotinus, 1956: Ennead 5.7). Here is the eternal in the finite, and where the path and goal are the same, there eternity enters the Now, so that every moment is eternal and peaceful and at rest. This is *Fruition*, which concerns quality, in contrast to modern economics' 'endless *Progress*' measured in quantity.

Like Plato, Boethius assumed that society should be governed by the Good. It is interesting therefore to see how secularism has taken over the idea of the Good and applied it to consumerism as 'goods'. In this, the spiritual qualitative element has been reduced to a material quantity, whereas Boethius' 'Good' applies to the life of virtue, to which the possession of material things can be an impediment. Indeed, the economic emphasis in the *Consolation* is on experiential and embodied values rather than material riches. This rebalancing of spirit and body, quality and quantity, is what is needed in contemporary economics, and this is exactly what the oikos is designed to supply: an adequate economy that covers basic needs while supporting the vitality of the individual and social institutions.

Evil

Animals adapt well to their native ecosystem, but if the animal nature in the human dominates, this opposes the higher order of nature. This conflict between a higher and lower nature is eloquently expressed in a letter written in Greek to the church in Rome by the apostle Paul five centuries prior to Boethius' residence in Rome:

'For I do not do the good I want, but the evil I do not want is what I do. Now if I do what I do not want, it is no longer I that do it, but sin which dwells in me. So I find it to be a law that when I want to do the right, evil lies close at hand. For I delight in the law of God, in my inmost self, but I see in my members another law at war with the law of my mind and making me captive to the law of sin which dwells in my members." (Romans 7, 19–23, Revised Standard Version).

Society and its economy have to deal with this conflict. If the world is essentially Good, with a Good helmsman (C 4.1.11) it would seem that, assuming that the purpose of humanity is progression towards divinity, that this will require various resistances for virtue to overcome. This falling short of the Good and allowing the animal nature to dominate is a persistent theme in the *Consolation*. Boethius asserts that Man's vocation, or rightful relationship to reality is to participate in the Good, and anyone who departs from this is committing sin. For a being with a mind made in the image of God, turning from the path governed by Providence (the telos of the Good), implies, according to Philosophia, that one's mind reverts to that of an animal governed by desire rather than virtue.

If the desire for pleasure – Plato's eros/stomach category – is dominant instead of enthusiasm for virtue as a just stance towards reality, the result is disorder and incompletion that lacks true happiness. Harmony between the three aspects of the soul (as in Plato's *Republic*) requires government by the head/reason: *Logistikon* is gentle rule within 'chest' and 'stomach' through love of learning. This threefold aspect of oikos as the whole, distinguishes itself distinctly from modern economics profit motivation, which can be seen as a false path characterized by incompletion, reducing happiness to consumption. If the Good is everything (as the whole) then going against it is denying one's nature, denying the continuity between Nature and human nature. Such action can be called evil because it is contrary to the Good. But the terms: 'evil', 'wicked', and 'bad' are not tightly defined by Boethius and merge into one another; yet the point is that what is contrary to the Good can be seen as evil.

The Christian perspective is that evil is real but not substantial,[14] and that it has its role within the whole, but is limited as a part within the scope of the whole. Boethius was in prison under sentence of death because, as he said, he entered politics, inspired by Plato's *Republic* to contribute to the Good, but false witness against him led to the charge of treason and sacrilege. For him, this represented Fortune turning against him, but this can also be seen as the result of evil. In this case, evil has power over the body but not over the soul (Self), as similarly the Wheel of Fortune has power over life on the earth, but this power does not extend beyond the death of the body. The soul (the home of the human) is the oikos, which obeys the law of balance between extremes (Aristotle's definition of virtue), and in the oikos the needs of the soul are balanced with those of the animal, where the spirit (reason) within the soul remains in control. But if *epithymeikon* (the pleasure principle) takes control, as is possible within modern economics (Aristotle's *chremastistics* as wealth creation), then the animal rules. Indeed, the animal is positive in its rightful place but when it opposes the Good it becomes evil.

However, evil lacks power in comparison with the Good. Philosophia even says that evil is 'nothing', since it has no existence as such due to departure from its connection with Being. Evil also has no real power to alter the Good. The oikos-soul is self-sufficient, founded on the virtues. This does not mean that evil is unreal, since it is a necessary part of the whole but it is limited in scope and redeemable. Boethius' insights are often expressed by reversing values. For example, he says that goodness is its own reward and likewise, wickedness is the punishment of the wicked (C 4.3.31–32).[15] As a category, the term 'wickedness' could be applied to the modern economy that appeals to the vices of human nature in direct contrast to the motivation towards the Good, particularly in the wealth creation sector where financial activity lacks a moral guiding compass. Philosophia regards the sin of departure from the true human path as failure and mental sickness, where evil is less an affliction than a deep infection. While weakness is a disease of the body, wickedness is seen as a disease of the mind, so that where the sick in body deserve sympathy, those who suffer from evil deserve pity rather than blame.

The Wheel of Fortune

While there is apparent injustice in a world subject to the Wheel of Fortune, Philosophia distinguishes between luck and uncertainty and in doing so reveals the difference between a worldly and other worldly viewpoint. In the opening scene of *Consolation*, Boethius complains about the injustice of his situation; this is not meant to justify resentment morality, but rather here is an example where resentment is sublimated by means of introspection, and where justice consists in remembering one's True nature. Boethius therefore discovers that justice is active in the present in the oikos as soul.

The Wheel of Fortune that features in Boethius' *Consolation* is a widely celebrated image. It emphasizes the major part played in life by luck and chance. Indeed, while it is possible to insure against risk, insurance will not cover everything. Yet a feature of the oikos is that the injustice of Fortune is redeemable through philosophy's consolation, which pits the lawfulness of nature and virtue against the inconstancy of Fortune. This is Law versus Luck where opposites are held in parallel as a means of integration and balance to arrive at stability within change and fortune.[16] According to Philosophia, adverse fortune can turn men back to their true good, so bad luck can have the effect of turning people to the Truth, and Justice is met if basic needs are satisfied.

The inconstancy of Fortune cannot, however, keep pace with a person's insatiable greed (C 2.2.29–30), and it is irrational to argue for insatiable greed in a world shared by everyone (C 2.2.48–50). In a finite world, infinite greed promotes inequality and strife. This is where the basic needs oikos, with its built-in equity, is superior to the materialist consumer economy. In his book, *Elegant Simplicity*, Satish Kumar speaks of owning few possessions but beautiful ones that can be cherished and enjoyed, as opposed to a clutter of possessions that invoke anxiety and can 'own' their owner. Living simply requires attention, awareness, and mindfulness, emphasizing the distinction between having and being.

Natural Ethics

A craving for more is a sign of insufficiency, revealing a state of poverty (C 2.m2.18–19). One's true wealth is in knowing that one is a human being, with all the dignity this implies.

Nature is described as content with little, and a direct link is suggested between the facts of nature and norms. Indeed, Natural Ethics reasons from nature to values and hence to values rooted in nature. The nature considered here includes human nature. This is a holistic view of nature rather than a modern nature that is opposed to culture. Nature is defined here in the ancient sense of 'physis' and Being. This incorporates the Good so that 'nature' is the opposite of base animal nature. Nature is not infinite, and so infinite growth and consumption are antithetic to nature. Erich Fromm (1900–1980) thought that we need to develop a natural ethics derived from human nature (Fromm, 1994), and economist K. William Kapp (1910–1976) similarly argued that norms can be derived from basic human needs

(Kapp, 1985). The natural ethics of the oikos relate to the finite world, but are nourished by virtues, which are timeless. Here, the world of the finite and the infinite integrate and in doing so enact the mystery of the oikos. This value base distinguishes the oikos from the 'value-free' positive character of modern economics based on abstract calculation.

Fortune's inconstancy can serve a higher purpose when constant change maintains harmony (C 2.m8.1–2). In as much as this harmony is maintained by Love, so Fortune in the form of Fate is subject to Providence supported by Divine Love. There is an association here with Empedocles' *Love* and *Strife* (the tendency to draw together and pull apart) as forces governing the physical elements. This is Natural Law underpinned by Divine Providence: the continuity of the Divine into the material world. Such an idea of harmony applies to the oikos in terms of justice and proportion contributing to the Good.[17] This insight advances the need for an adequate economy to meet genuine human needs without harming other beings and the environment. Just such an economy is demonstrated in Buddhist Economics, advocated by Ernst Schumacher (1911–1977) in *Small is Beautiful: a Study of Economics as if People Mattered* (1973).[18]

Buddhist economics is an example of the continued relevance of *Consolation*'s oikos, where focus is directed to interdependence between human beings and Nature, with emphasis on 'right livelihood' and creative human work, rather than on machine production, in realization that creativity enhances the human. What is harmful is clearly distinguished from what is beneficial in the production and consumption of goods and services. Bhutan is an example of a Buddhist economy where instead of GNP as a measure of the economy, GNH (Gross National Happiness) is applied as a measure of human well-being. Here, it is a question of not multiplying human wants, but of purification of human character. Karma Ura, President from 1999 of the *Centre for Bhutan Studies and GNH Research*, has promoted this approach, which is an important contribution to alternatives to mainstream neoliberal economics. This is an example of Heterodox Economics. Karma Ura was interviewed in *What is Heterodox Economics: Interviews with leading economists* (Mearman, 2019).

Defining an economy in Boethius' terms means prioritizing the production of useful goods over items that indulge vanity and animal passions. Here, the socialist ideas of William Morris from the nineteenth century are relevant. In looking back to medieval craftsmanship, Morris yearned for beauty in everyday products in contrast to uniform machine production. He wanted working-energy to be applied in 'useful work' and not in 'useless toil'. However, his attempts to practice this within an Arts and Crafts movement were frustrated by the dominant system of capitalist industrial production. Indeed, capitalism has its place in supplying human needs but under some circumstances can harm human welfare.

When a profane view supersedes a sacred attitude to life this enables materialism to dominate society, and this mood in turn will promote an economy of consumption with all its associated side effects and impediments to well-being. But the basic-needs oikos of *Consolation* leads to normative decision-making on social priorities concerning well-being of the soul as the dwelling place of the human.

b. The Wealth of Happiness

Consolation defines wealth as 'inner treasure'. This implies that having an overriding concern for money constitutes pursuit of a false Good, because this deflects awareness from the Creator as the source of one's being and inner wealth. Philosophia recognizes that Boethius is sick because he has forgotten his True nature. To achieve the Good is to *realize* human nature by participating in the Divine, and True happiness is to recognize one's inner divinity.

From this point of view, it is possible to attain completion or Self-realization in this life through attaining the Good, which is a state of beatitude through participation in the Good by activating virtue. Possession of the knowledge that the true source of happiness is within means that happiness is under the control of the Self and so is independent of misfortune. This understanding of happiness as the Good, which is equivalent to the Truth, is a striking contrast to the neoliberal concept that Truth is rooted in the Market. Such a view undermines the Self.

Consolation prioritizes inner treasure over material possessions[19] on the basis that the spiritually nourished oikos develops goodness as happiness. This is experiential wealth in contrast to ownership of possessions in the belief that these offer true wealth. Boethius in fact embodied *Consolation*'s ideal of inner wealth with his inner compass directed toward philosophy, supported by the liberal arts of grammar, logic, rhetoric, mathematics, geometry, music and astronomy.[20] Inclusive of the joy of being made in the image of God,[21] Boethius had the wealth of the soul's potential capacity for mystical union with the Good, the Divine; as a Christian he would be assured that the kingdom of heaven is within. However, while he apparently lived a virtuous life, it was only much later when reflecting in prison that he realized that he had in fact valued riches and status. This was a significant fault in him, yet it is not that enjoyment of wealth and reputation is wrong, but that his priority had wandered away from the Good. For him true poverty would be neglect of the mind, and spiritual starvation of the soul, which effectively lacks oiko-nomia. Indeed while his imprisonment might seem like poverty, he occupies it by creating for his soul, and posterity, inestimable riches in the *Consolation.*

True wealth is associated with the soul: it is transcendental as well as embodied in character developed through virtue. This is the oikos as the dwelling place of the human. It facilitates true happiness as the wealth of beatitude. The inherited wealth of likeness to God (C 2.5.48) is experiential wealth, and this form of *virtue ethics*[22] must be distinguished from modern *decision ethics* based on the utilitarian principles of maximizing gain. *Consolation*'s wealth is based on the pursuit and attainment of the Good in contrast to the utilitarian calculus of exchange values. Indeed if pursuit of material wealth is prioritized over the development of a virtuous life this constitutes false wealth, an illusion of riches that can be lost with a change in fortune, because it is not owned in the same way that character is part of one's Self. In contrast to material values, virtue and character have soul-spiritual (eternal) value. Philosophia argues that everyone seeks happiness (as human wealth) but they do so in ways that can be false paths. True wealth is in the oikos, which is infused with living spirit, whereas an economy of purely worldly wealth is subject to the 'wheel of fortune', and in this respect is hollow. To gain the whole world and lose, one's soul (one's true home) would be loss indeed in spite of apparent gain.

Philosophia says that people are blind to where their true good lies. They seek on earth that which transcends the merely earthly (C 3.m8.15–18).

> Sed quonam lateat quod cupiunt bonum
> Nescire caeci sustinent
> Et quod stelliferum trans abiit polum
> Tellure demersi petunt. (Boethius, 2014: 77, 29-32)

It is a mistake to equate money with wealth because money is just a token. Real wealth is nature and a rich experience of life. This includes the capacity for enthusiasm, good health and a sense of wonder, and participation in a living universe. True wealth includes freedom, imagination, friendship, community, love, joy, beauty, creativity, happiness, and activity suited to one's disposition. This is where the need categories of Max Neef are relevant.

A modern Quaker attitude endorses Boethius' idea of self-sufficiency and the need for divine awareness to be applied in the economy:

> All is One. The material world is at the same time the field of mysticism – the union of mind and heart with the external reality underlying all that exists, the ultimate fulfilment of love and Truth. . . . But beyond this, the compelling convention of our time is to separate and divide;

> and sometimes we allow this to take over our thoughts and words, in such a way that, almost unknowingly, we too, separate everyday matters from divine discourse. . . . I want to propose, that we need, once more, to reclaim this notion of wholeness or 'holiness' as part of our everyday lives now; to suggest that without this common experience and remembrance something will always be missing; to suggest that the absence of wholeness and holiness leaves us incomplete and empty both within ourselves and with our neighbours near and far.
>
> (Cadman, 2010: 1, 4)

The view expressed here affirms the need for daily life to be affected by theological belief: becoming one with 'what is' through participation in the Good, which participates Creation. Such a view supports the idea that we can only be truly ourselves when we act in accordance with Eternal and Natural law. Love is the executive power and Providence is the guiding principle. This recognizes that we are part of a greater whole and participate in its fulfilment. This means acting for the good of all and accepting the natural rhythms of life and death. Such an attitude acknowledges ancient and medieval wisdom, which prioritizes knowledge of Being, where 'telos' draws towards perfection (the fullness of Being), with 'Eros' as the yearning towards the highest actuality. Since the *intellect* is the divine part, which defines the human being, contemplation of Truth generates, according to Aristotle, the greatest happiness. If this attitude is adopted more widely it would create in accordance a demand to re-root modern economics in the oikos, and consequently challenge mere consumerism and the profit-motive as insufficient, and a totally inadequate vision for a holistic and just society.

The goals of oikos and the modern economy represent two different visions that lead towards two different ends. The oikos should lead to mutuality and harmony in society, because its reliance on cooperation means that competition is largely eliminated, whereas the modern neoliberal economy encourages self-interest, which potentially leads to separation and isolation from reality as a whole. Apart from this, the effect of the happiness gained through participation in the Good (the common good) maintains an authentic *quality* that is lacking in modern economics that bases its happiness on transient pleasure. Such happiness is illusory relative to happiness resulting from a felt relationship to the whole, manifesting as the Good.[23]

c. The Poverty of Hoarding

Philosophia presents four economic ideas (C 2.5.7–18): hoarded money as power; spending as winning a favourable reputation; money as gift is valuable; and inequality is produced by money accumulated by individuals.

Fortunately a gift culture exists today as charitable giving, and the moral wealth of giving is an experiential social value. Within the oikos, generosity is a virtue in comparison with trading. The idea that money has value while in circulation (C 2.5.13–14) suggests that an economic system is less like a mechanism and more like a living organic process. If money is to function within an organic process it also needs to decay in value over time equivalent to the goods for which it is a token, otherwise it is out of step with the reality of its associated living situation. The economy is a social provisioning process and the amount of money in circulation should reflect this. Silvio Gesell's proposal for the regular depreciation of the face value of money is intended to discourage hoarding (Eisenstein, 2011: 209). Gasell's ideas for a higher average wage and zero interest were proposed in the interest of material equality. Money is a token invested with spirit (intellect), and spirit is characterized by *movement*, so decay over time in the value of money will discourage hoarding and encourage economic activity, and in this way maintain a healthy circulation of goods and services. Money invested in land ownership is also a form of hoarding; therefore, the financial value of land should also be subjected to the principle of decay over time in a similar way to congealed capital, because income from land rent is equivalent to an interest payment on hoarded capital.

The accumulation of money is a form of hoarding even when spent in financial transactions on the stock exchange when it could instead enter into the real economy of production of physical assets. Implied here is the idea that money is withdrawn from the real economy through financial speculation. Indeed when the differential between the rich and the poor becomes very great this threatens to disrupt any remaining harmony in society. When this happens, the economy needs to be adjusted to meet a just distribution of the monetary wealth, which is actually created primarily through ownership of land and technology embodied in capital. Georgism addresses this question of justice through the distribution of tax by arguing for a tax on ground rent gained from land ownership (economic rent), particularly in relation to valuable urban locations.

Georgism argues for a 'Land Value Tax' that can be used to reduce or eliminate unfair and inefficient taxes on income, housing, trade, and purchases. The concept of a land tax has a long tradition starting with Adam Smith, and had been endorsed philosophically by John Locke and Spinoza before Henry George popularized it in his book, *Progress and Poverty (George, 1879)*. Movement toward equity can confidently be achieved through a redistributive tax system applied to land ownership and accumulated money. Another solution to monetary inequality is democratization of the means of production, where part-ownership of machines and democratic decision-making can lead to a wider distribution of profits. This provides an economic solution to material inequality. Here, virtue as *justice* overrides the lower animal motive of *greed.* According to the economist, Yanis Varoufakis, a moral choice is presented between 'democratizing' or 'commodifying' everything, including the management of money, technology, and the planet's ecosystems and resources.[24]

Hoarding certainly interrupts the flow of money and contributes to the gulf between rich and poor (C 2.5.21–22). However, in our excessively technological society based on division of labour, security provided by personal savings can be justified, but these 'savings' would be superfluous if a basic income was guaranteed, and basic needs were covered by public utilities. Another form of hoarding is where capitalists and rentiers extract a surplus that by right belongs to the worker. Apart from this, if greed is encouraged within an economy based on interest-bearing loans and money created as debt, a society based on the principle of 'have now and pay later' ultimately condemns its citizens to unhappiness in the long term when accrued debt becomes too great to repay, with all of its associated repercussions. People who enter into debt as a result of an inability to pay household expenses highlight a social problem that the modern economy fails to adequately address. On the other hand, the oikos of basic needs distinguishes between basic *needs* and created *wants*, with the aim of satisfying limited and finite human needs.

Another form of poverty is time, and as artificial intelligence increasingly impacts the world of work and leisure, this provides an opportunity for people to be released from the treadmill of 'jobs', and, if provided with a citizen's dividend (an allowance) people can redirect their work to their interests and to 'useful work', including the immediate concerns of humanity such as environmental maintenance and care within the community. This requires organization, but successful coordination and cooperation between free individuals in voluntary organizations and in civil society has an established track record. As a social anarchist, Peter Kropotkin liked to quote the English Lifeboat Association as an example of exemplary voluntary self-organization.[25] Obviously payment of a citizen's wage involves a re-evaluation of work and economic needs, but increasing crises may force this re-evaluation on society.

If 'progress' away from the idea of God and towards mechanism and a smart artificial world means departure from Goodness, Beauty and Truth (nourished by the Divine), then our progressive 'gain' will be a great loss, resulting in emasculation of the soul, effectively amounting to the sacrifice of richness on the altar of poverty. No amount of money will save the soul if it is invested in self-interest, but the redirection of money in conformity with the principle of justice aligns itself with the vision of the Good. Philanthropy is to be encouraged through foundations and through wills, but a form of tax may provide a better guarantee that the public purpose will be served. Without such a vision, spiritual poverty will seriously endanger the prospect of a continuing meaningful human culture and civilization.

d. Nature and Spirit

The ancient world needs to be understood in its own terms, for it represents a form of consciousness that has been largely superseded, or lost today. For Plato and Aristotle there was an ethical dimension to knowledge because knowledge of the Truth of things involved correspondence between the integrity of human nature and the order of Nature (Milne, 2013: 25). Also for Plato and Aristotle, the idea of order, or cosmos, meant justice between all things, and chaos meant misrule. In this ancient understanding, the cosmic order was divinely directed and so was not a mechanism devoid of an ethical dimension. Indeed the universe was considered to be virtuous. This is a strange idea for a modern person to accept, given modernity's acceptance of materialism. How spirit and nature interact in the balanced soul to form the oikos is mysterious, and philosophy's consolation illuminates the mystery of this economy. If oikos is the balanced soul, then the economy is the mystery through which nature and spirit find balance in the soul. Here, we have what may be called a 'poetic economy', where the nature of the human being is central and where the soul is the intermediary between spirit and body, the heavenly and the earthly.

Although it may not be possible or even advisable to revert to an ancient *participatory* mode of consciousness, which to some extent extended into the medieval period, it is possible to reconnect to the flow of reality (nature) by means of a form of post-modern participation through the use of poetic imagination to bridge the subject-object divide caused by the domination of the modern intellect, and to re-integrate morality into the world of material reality. This requires the use of active imagination to re-establish the subject's participation in the object (as idea) at a consciously willed level.[26] Owen Barfield identifies this need in his book, *Saving the Appearances*, which examines the evolution of consciousness. He speaks of a lost world that needs to be regained if incalculable disaster is to be avoided (Barfield, 1988: 85).

What modernity overlooks or fails to understand about the ancient world is its conception of Nature as *energia*: active being or being as action in process. Nature is both Being and Thing, and the ancients distinguished within Nature between '*naturans*' as active and '*naturata*' as the passive completion of the process of naturans.[27] An analytic intellect cannot grasp this living activity of 'naturans' in its own terms, but poetic imagination, which is mobile as 'energia', can participate with Nature in its process as verb (as in a state of becoming). Where the one-sided intellect of the subject divides subject from object, imagination can reconnect subject and object in a consciously willed way. An example of this use of imagination is Goethe's 'natural-humane' or 'poetic-scientific' method demonstrated in his *Metamorphosis of Plants*.[28] This is an important point because our attitude to nature determines whether it is treated as a living system or as a world of things to be exploited.

A key difference between the oikos of *Consolation* and modern neoclassical economics is between an economy that in principle is organic (adjusting in a living way to circumstances) and concerned with the holistic welfare of a household, as against a mechanistic economy based on the calculus of utility and profit maximization. In addition to the ancient world's distinctly different attitude to the natural world, *Consolation* also regards Nature as a Divine Creation. The pre-Socratic philosopher, Empedolces, understood Nature to be composed of four 'states of matter' exhibiting the qualities of earth, water, air, and fire. Similarly a relationship was observed to exist between human nature and Nature. Plato spoke of a World Soul that animates nature.[29] Indeed, it is through the human soul that a felt relationship can be established with Nature. Nature nurtures humanity with its rich resources.

The constantly changing world remains in balance and the battling elements maintain peace (C 2.m8.1–4).

> Quod mundus stabili fide
> Concordes uariat uices,
> Quod pugnantia semina
> Foedus perpetuum tenant. (Boethius, 2014: 55, 12-15)

This passage refers to the physics of Empedocles with its theory of the four states of matter that, when mixed and separated by Love and Strife, constitute Nature. According to W. P. Ker, Boethius was often nearer to Parmenides or Empedocles in his frame of mind if not in his doctrines (Ker, 1955: 115).

The ancient Greek term 'physis' (nature) has an association with the verb, 'growing'. Indeed, early Greek philosophy enquired into the order of nature where natural objects were conceived as 'essencing forth'. Nature was understood as a principle of growth and to be distinguished from artificial things. Drawing upon Plato, *Consolation* presents nature as Divine Creation sustained by the Good, and this divine and living dimension of nature means that land is a source of subsistence as well as the gift of God. It is for this reason that the tradition of *physiocracy* (government of nature) recognizes that wealth is generated solely from nature. This contrasts with the modern conception of Nature as essentially a resource to be economically exploited. However, recent thinking in response to global warming emphasizes the ecological dimension of Nature, and the need for sustainable development. This reflects the pre-Socratic understanding of nature as an ordered system and, as we now understand it, interconnected ecosystems within the overall ecosystem of the earth and cosmos.

The self-sufficient oikos of *Consolation* combines a sustainable and renewable economy with Plotinus' ideal of transcendental union with the One. Here, nature and spirit combine to support the Good life, where fruition is True happiness. Re-rooting the economy in this oikos will therefore help to restore awareness of the sacred dimension to nature, and in turn support the cause of sustainability and concern for the environment. Also contained within the oikos of *Consolation* is the idea of the stewardship of nature as a sacred duty and responsibility. Sustainable development implies not only the survival of humanity but also a right relationship to reality, to the Whole (the Good), and this relates to human destiny. *Consolation*'s oiko-nomia, based on Nature in the sense of 'physis' in its relation to Being and the Whole, is therefore a self-sufficient, sustainable, and renewable economy.

We find in experience that an economy based on the profit motive leads to commodification of land and labour. 'Goods' have become commodities and in the process their intrinsic *spiritual or experiential value* has been replaced by their *exchange value*. Anything that cannot be made into a marketable commodity is regarded as of no economic value. This means that the spiritual and the use-value that the oikos recognizes are ignored in the market calculus based on prices. This stark difference in values is connected with the fundamental shift away from ancient metaphysics to a modern age characterized by an egocentric calculus and the maximization of utility and profits.

Land is vital to health and well-being in human dwelling in the form of gardens, allotments, and leisure activity including sport and exercise. For this reason sufficient land needs to be owned by public bodies and trusts.[30] Examples of this do exist, for example, in the National Trust in the UK, and the National Parks in North America. Leisure spent in the natural environment is life-enhancing and nourishes the spirit. If Nature is to nourish humanity, then equality of access is needed, otherwise only a few will reap the benefits of this experiential wealth.

God's 'mind' is spirit, which is seeded into the human being: Philosophia says that minds descend from divine regions to be enclosed in earthly bodies (C 3.m6.5). The vital distinction to be made here between the human and Nature is that the essential identity of humankind is connected to what is 'on high'. The spiritual and the material combine in the human being in living union, and the spirit, soul, and body are equally important in the oikos. They mutually support each other as they do in the human organism when in a state of *good* health. Additionally Nature as physis, which provides Law, Measure, and Ethics, equally provides measure to the oikos. Natural Theology, based on the lawfulness of nature, is Natural Law. Nature is not inferior to spirit (mind), but is different in essence. Nature constitutes the physical world for the incarnated human spirit, yet there is mutual dependence, and human responsibility to maintain a right relationship to reality (the whole), which includes stewardship of Nature. Continuity between Nature and human nature is also apparent when Nature is thought of as culture, because it is by means of human cognition that nature becomes a phenomenon. Acknowledging 'physis' as encapsulating the invisible laws behind nature, C. S. Lewis commented incisively that while the cardinal problem for ancient wisdom was to conform the soul to reality (achieved through knowledge, self-discipline, and virtue), for magic and applied science, the problem was how to subdue reality to the wishes of man (Lewis, 1962: 52).

This distinction made by C. S. Lewis is significant because the intention of *Consolation* is to conform the soul to reality. In this regard, the meaning of economy is the balancing process of the soul. Conforming to reality in economic terms will therefore include cooperation between human reason and the intelligence of Nature realized through sustainable environmental projects, and development of organic methods of food production, instead of reliance on industrial approaches that assault and violate nature. Unfortunately the tendency with technology that is governed by the profit motive is to mechanize life itself, and this has to be recognized if survival of an independent human spirit is valued. Here, the common element between Nature and human nature is significant, since the experience of living resonance is qualitatively different from an abstract, mechanistic, and technological relationship (or disconnection) to Nature. The attitude of *war* against 'weeds' and 'pests' could be re-rooted into concerted cooperation with the genius of Nature. Objective morality underpins a divinely ordered world where Goodness rooted in God is the means by which the divine becomes manifest in the world.

Boethius was deeply attached to the Neoplatonic conception of the universe as a living whole where universal intelligence unites the human with the cosmos. Neoplatonism also viewed reality as a hierarchy of communicating levels. The origin of all was conceived as 'One', from which emanated *Intellect* and then *Soul*.[31] Nature was seen as a further emanation, then a sequence of levels followed, constituting an intelligent and harmonious order. Boethius therefore understood Nature to be animated by soul, making Nature a living entity characterized by movement. In this case as God's living creation, Nature demands our deepest respect, and it is essential that this respectful attitude to nature is acknowledged in the environmental debate concerning the degradation of the planet.

At present, the modern economic process contributes to environmental destruction, but if nature is left intact in many cases, it could have more value to the whole than when processed for economic gain. This is particularly evident in the case of the Amazon Rainforest where its value to climate sustainability, with the forest's significant ability to remove and store carbon from the atmosphere implicated in the rise in global temperature, needs to be set against short-term economic gain from logging. Also the use of the cleared land can be outweighed by the universal benefit of a sustainable planet. In view of climate change, economic development needs to be maintained at a sustainable level suited to environmental regeneration. In this respect, traditional organic agriculture (not to be confused with farming for profit) not only respects the environment but is more economic in the long term. In some contexts, conservation may be opposed to agriculture, but it is important to get the balance of priorities right because organic agriculture can provide not only vitality in healthy food but also healthy and wholesome employment. This is preferable to factory and industrial farming that creates monocultures needing industrial chemical support with fertilizers and pesticides, which then deplete the soil quality, resulting in nutrient-poor food. Such a system is unsustainable and adds to climate change through waste products, air pollution, and consumption of fuel in the process. This creates a future economic burden while destabilizing the harmony of the planet on which life depends. The idea of the biodynamic farm is relevant here, since it is in effect a complete and sustainable ecosystem in itself, providing an oikos integrated into the cosmic whole.[32]

Earthly material substance is fundamental in meeting bodily needs but it is spirit as intelligence that organizes the economic process, so that a product is essentially a combination of spirit and matter. Spiritual intelligence enters into design and production techniques that inform the product. The intelligent spirit also participates in the distribution process and the practical economy relies on human relationships where producers, distributors, and consumers are able to decide what human needs can be met by the economy. Of course, this need not exclude market exchange for need satisfaction. In this way, the spiritual and material work in harmony. The practical economy of oikos is not an abstract economy that operates independently from human life, but on the contrary directly reflects human relationships and values as a combination of spirit and matter. The role of spirit in the economic process is active; it acts on passive material, providing it with a form suited to human flourishing.

e. The Part and the Whole

Consolation understands Nature to be the creation of God where the Good acts from within creation as its telos. This makes it possible to understand Divinity as both beyond and within Creation (Panentheism), so that transcendental union in the oikos as the *well-balanced soul* makes for a mysterious economy designed to achieve human fruition. This qualitative soul value distinguishes the oikos from the modern utilitarian economy where a mechanistic and maximizing calculus determines price (exchange value) that reflects the usefulness or goodness of a thing. Essentially the difference here is between *living Being* and *Thing*, where being is incalculable (a gift through Creation) and price is precisely calculable, enabling the calculus of modern economics to know the price of everything but the True value of nothing.

Consolation's values concern virtuous pursuit of the Good as the Whole. The relationship of the part to the whole matters, because, as a part, the soul or oikos is open to the whole which nourishes and sustains it. Without this relationship, it would be autonomous and abstract, and tyrannical in relation to the whole. This distinction reveals the radical difference between oikos and the modern neoclassical vision of an atomized, individualistic world of material consumption where growth in Gross Domestic Product is the primary objective, and the human is an abstract 'agent' pursuing self-interest by optimizing maximum utility within a narrowly defined world of exchange values. Indeed, maximization of utility is based on a mechanistic view of the world that works with *defined* forces, in contrast to *Consolation*'s *living* world of Being. The vision held by modern economics is that of a detached technocratic system that ignores human concerns like general well-being, human rights, job security, and mental health. On the contrary, it is the concern of the self-sufficient oikos as well-balanced soul, to furnish a household in the world for the human to feel physically, psychologically, and spiritually at home.

The unity of Nature reveals itself in the totality of its living intelligent quality where all parts interconnect within the living whole. God's power binds the whole together, which includes everything that exists. A vital aspect of the 'One' (God) is understood to inhere in each part, interconnecting each part and the individual parts to the whole.[33] The oikos, as well-balanced and integrated soul, is open to the Whole, and oiko-nomia means taking on Truth and Goodness as attributes of the Whole. Microcosm connects with macrocosm, which is the transcendental aspect of the oikos enabling the soul, or Self, to contain inner wealth. In contrast, a value-based market economy displaces this divine law and effectively regards money as God, so replacing God with money. This creates instability and conflict.

According to *Consolation*, a good household is self-sufficient in its oikos when it participates in the Good as the whole in its transcendental character of opening to the One. Participation in the whole, in the One, leads to self-sufficiency by inclusion in the whole. This enables us to see economics not in isolation but as interconnected within the whole of Reality. An economy that isolates itself from the whole must be judged by the fruit that it bears.

Completing the Circle

Philosophia sings of soul encircling mind (C 3.m9.16). This is the World Soul that circles the Mind of God, and similarly the human soul circles the human mind in microcosmic reflection. God is the centre, and Divinity pervades the circle from centre to circumference. This suggests that the Whole is concerned with completing the circle within the soul-oikos through a mysterious economy constituted by reason, poetic reflection, and love, in order to achieve fruition through the Good. According to Plotinus the soul is not a circle in the sense of a geometric figure but in the sense that it contains the Primal Nature (as centre), and is contained by it (as circumference), and owes its origin to such a centre (Plotinus, 1948: 217).

The Consolation of Philosophy also points to anamnesis for self-sufficiency from philosophy. Here, the immanence of the eternal Self in the still-centre can be experienced as completion within passing time, offering fullness in the present within a finite life. Additionally Boethius presents 'telos' in such a way to show that eternity exerts a compelling influence on daily life. Here, participation in the whole can yield consciousness of *fruition* as the *eternal* realized in the present. This notion is affirmed by the Japanese philosopher, Kitaro Nishida, with his view that the goal of true religion should lie in grasping eternal life in its own immediacy in our lives (Kitaro, 1993: 115). Additionally, the theologian, Paul Tillich, expressed the view that when time is experienced without the 'eternal now', it is mere transitoriness without the actual presence of Being (Tillich, 1957: 79).

Time relates to eternity as part to the whole (C 5.3). As a measure of change, time is organic: it cannot be reversed, unlike in mechanics that is subject to timelessness, having no history or qualitative change. Similarly, modern economics is timeless, based as it is on money as a unit of account that is not subject to the natural organic cycle that includes decay. There is a link here with the First Law of Thermodynamics where energy in the universe is held to be constant and unchanging. But Fortune unfolds in time, making for a probabilistic universe (C 4.6). This applies to modern science, which relies on chance events. So when modern science and modern economics treat the finite as if infinite (timeless), this represents a disconnection from lived reality.

Infinite desire in a finite world is logically unsustainable. This demonstrates the advantage that the self-sufficient oikos has over modern economics driven by the motive of infinite growth in Gross Domestic Product. Based on Aristotle's notion of chremastistics, modern economics differs dramatically from the oikos largely based on Natural Law. Oikos is rooted in Nature as the Good that delivers inner quality, and not in a false Good that produces inner poverty. Significantly, *Consolation's* oikos also has the potential to redeem infinite desire by sublimating it into the desire for virtue instead of desire for goods. When modern economics dismisses ancient wisdom and adheres strictly to calculation, it overlooks the fact that Wealth of Being is self-sufficient and so leaves nothing further to be desired.

While the five means of achieving happiness (fame, wealth, status, power, and pleasure) are incomplete as separate aims, according to Philosophia when brought together in unison they lack nothing so that as a whole they equate to the Good. This suggests the possibility of a circling home where infinite desire is redeemed through the wholeness of self-sufficiency so that modern economics is transformed into the inner wealth of the oikos.

Knowledge

Philosophia says that a multiplicity of kinds of knowledge is given to different substances (C 5.5.10–11). This multiplicity can be visualized as a great 'chain of being' where differences in knowledge and capacities exist within a continuum from the very highest to the very least in the universe. God's knowledge as omniscience is the highest capacity and unimaginable from a human standpoint, since, as Philosophia says, it embraces past, present, and future in a permanent Now. This implies that God *is* omniscience rather than that God *has* omniscience. She says that every object of knowledge is known not of its own nature, but of the nature of those who comprehend it (C 5.6.1–3).

Aristotle expressed the idea that the essence of something cannot be fully known unless the same pattern (Form) is available in the mind to match the Form of the object. *Like is known by like* so that only a virtuous mind can know that which is virtuous. This is objective knowledge as distinct from subjectivism or relativism. Human intelligence, as a divine capacity, interconnects with Divine Intelligence (as part with the whole). Aside from this, there is differentiation in the human being between reason, imagination, and perception. This rich variation in human capacity, to which feeling and volition must be added, is reduced in modern economic discourse to the single dimension of information processing and calculus, which ignores the very reason for an economy based on the oikos as the balanced soul. As such, economics based on information and reductionism cannot provide an economy fit for the human soul. Knowledge is a vital factor in human free choice.[34]

Arguably an era develops its own metaphysical image, and this is expressed in an appropriate political structure. In a dominantly secular, science-based, materialist culture that we find ourselves in any movement toward a holistic (Good) conception of life might require a crisis to provide a space and opportunity for renewal of the political structure in order to support an oikos that can satisfy general human needs. *Consolation*'s self-sufficient oikos is a dramatic contrast to an economy allied to a mechanistic conception where separate parts contribute to a whole without the participation of the whole in the parts. This mechanistic atomization that determines modern economics leads, apart from separation and alienation, to an inability to adequately appreciate the whole. An instrumental and mechanistic worldview compromises and destroys the living qualities evident in Nature, and as such represents the thoughtlessness of the animal in man, which allows the adoption of vitality-destroying technologies to be applied towards devastation of the essentially human, and the earthly environment.

Love

While the totality of the wisdom in philosophy falls far short of the divine intelligence, the human capacity for reason can organize a workable economy, yet what such rationality might lack is *love*, which, like enthusiasm, empowers virtue in seeking the Good.

Blest are those who enthrone in their hearts the love that rules the sky (C 2.m8.28–30).

> O felix hominum genus,
> Si uestros animos amor
> Quo caelum regitur regat! (Boethius, 2014: 57, 3-5)

Love as a divine power in the universe is vitally needed in economics involving human relationships of association and mutuality. Such an economy can only be achieved meaningfully through friendship and respect. Love as Care is specifically addressed in *Feminist Economics* in its concern for family members in the household who are otherwise overlooked or taken for granted by neoclassical economics. Feminist economists argue that care-giving contributes to well-being and on this basis needs to be included in economic calculations. Feminist economic care for the environment supports 'degrowth' of the economy, a principle equally supported by *Ecological Economics*. Degrowth represents a political, economic and social movement based on ecological economics. It is anti-consumerist and anti-capitalist, with care at its centre.

Philosophia tells us that nature took its origin from that which is unimpaired and perfect, but it has degenerated into a fallen and worn out condition (C 3.10.13–16). However, Nature is a Good in providing all that is needed, even though it has fallen from perfection. However, there are economic activities that cause harm to the whole. These include mineral, gas, and oil extraction, an issue that is addressed in Nicholas Georgescu-Roegen's book: *The Entropy Law and the Economic Process*. In this book, Georgescu-Roegen applies the law of entropy to economics by assuming a limited supply of the earth's resources and their use as irrevocable, where low entropy (disorder) is transformed into the high entropy of decay. This continuing activity postulates a future where the world will no longer have any resources left and so can no longer support an economy, consequently endangering the prospect for human survival. Such a bleak prospect accentuates the need for Degrowth and Ecological Economics for the sake of human survival. Therefore, environmentally damaging extraction is best avoided where there are alternatives. Industrial agriculture that utilizes the earth's resources also increases entropy. In contrast, however, a caring attitude is revealed in the oikos based on renewable resources. According to Georgescu-Roegen, clinging to the model of linear progressive economic growth carries the prospect of death by incremental increases in entropy. What is needed is a regenerative circular natural system. An example would be where the interdependent nature of living systems can redirect sewage as a nutrient, thereby saving waste and obviating the need for artificial fertilizers. The argument for sustainability is compelling, and renewable energy (sun, wind, and water) in this scenario is much to be preferred to depletion of the earth's resources and global pollution in the pursuit of growth motivated by greed.

The idea of the Good as wholeness applies to Creation (Nature) as the Household of Humanity, and this greater household of the environment should be represented in economic accounting. This means bringing environmental costs into economic accounts for mining, and harvesting resources, and additionally the destruction caused by manufacturing processes that damage the environment. This should also apply to devastation caused by industrial methods of farming and fishing. Accounting for comprehensive environmental costs will reveal the economic advantage of strategies to sustain and renew, rather than to undermine the environment. For example, the annual loss of biodiversity and ecosystems has been estimated at almost twice the global annual GDP, according to a study published in the journal, *Nature* in 1997 (HRH, 2010: 73).

Continuous economic expansion has destabilized Earth's finely balanced and interconnected natural system (Gaia), resulting, among other things, in soil degradation, desertification, and climate change that affects weather patterns and sea levels due to melting reserves of ice. This situation urgently calls for sustainable and renewable development, which relates directly to the advantage of self-sufficient oikos. One example of a sustainable and self-sufficient community today is the Sekem settlement in Egypt.[35] This began as a project to reclaim an area of desert using biodynamic agriculture and has developed to support a large community with welfare facilities, educational training, and a university supporting equality and personal development in the community. An agricultural abundance enables produce to be supplied to the commercial market. This is an example of sustainable development that could be extended into a worldwide cooperative network for value creation. Everyone should have an equal right of access and use of the global commons of land, soil, water, and air. One of the ways of ensuring equality is through community or stakeholder management of constituent parts of the commons.

In order to flourish in today's world, people need *freedom*. This effectively means aligning individual purpose with Providence, which means relating to the Good and the Whole. Personal freedom includes the choice of fulfilling work where individual talent can be expressed while contributing to society. In this respect, it is important to reclaim the commons as a whole. It was enclosure policies that led to the ejection of people from land, creating a landless and impoverished, and easily manipulated populace. This policy interrupted a long tradition of the household being rooted in its own plot of land. Exceptional inequality is revealed in land ownership, and reallocation of land for general welfare is vital in a just society. An important option is for Land to be held in a trust and stewarded by the community for productive use.[36] Land ownership has to be considered in the light of humanity as a whole, taking into account ethics, justice, equality, liberty, responsibility, and mutuality.[37]

Associative Economics fits well with a participatory oikos where producers, distributors, and consumers confer in making joint decisions. It was Rudolf Steiner's view that economic life strives to structure itself according to its own nature, independent of politics and ideology, and it can only do this if associations, comprised of consumers, distributors and producers are established according to purely economic criteria, which are not laws but human beings using their immediate insights and interests to regulate the production, circulation and consumption of goods (Steiner, 1977: 17–18). Here, a 'fair price' remains important and arises in the process of value exchange. A fair price represents the relationship of values from the perspective of the producer, seller, and the buyer. This works well in the food supply chain where farmers, distributors and consumers each have a stake and a voice in the supply and price. If this stakeholder movement, with its holistic vision, replaced the shareholder business model, a spirit of cooperation, inclusion, and fellowship will arise in direct contrast to a mood of combative self-interest and exclusion.

Philosophia informs Boethius that he has learnt that all that exists is in a state of unity and that goodness is unity; therefore, everything that exists must be seen as good (C 4.3.39–42). In view of this, Boethius could hardly have imagined how far a future era might wander away from reason connected with the Good (the whole), to allow mechanistic thinking to apply to food production – a mode of thinking that is instrumental in destroying ecosystems through impoverishing soil and polluting the environment. Holistic reasoning recognizes that everything is connected within a web of life and that 'object-thinking' can lead to destructive procedures that ignore the living connectivity between organisms and ecosystems, where the 'object' is a subject in its own right. Ecological reasoning starts from the whole as the context in which the part has its being.

It becomes increasingly apparent with each crisis facing humanity that an oikos is needed that works in co-operation with Nature, and is embedded in the greater whole, as the soul is within God. Examples of this include Green Economics, which treats the economy as a component part of the total ecosystem in which it is embedded, and similarly Ecological Economics treats the economy as a subsystem of the larger ecosystem of the Earth. As such, they advocate both sustainable and renewable development and 'environmental full-cost accounting'. Yet contrary to the Ecological or Feminist Economics, Modern Economics utilizes nature, land, and people as economic factors and therefore fails to acknowledge their *real* value. Co-operation is needed to adjust imbalances and maintain harmony. The damage inflicted on the environment and on society by the reductive approach of modern neoliberal economics advances a convincing case for a more inclusive economics where different perspectives are taken into account that promote justice, morality and care. Other forms of economics may also prevent the rhythmic financial crises to which modern economics is subject in the way that it is tied to the Wheel of Fortune. A particularly important approach discussed by Tomas Sedlacek is Meta-economics. This is where the humanities offer contributions towards a fundamental understanding of economics and its purpose (Sedlacek, 2011/2013: 9). This is precisely the object of this study of *Consolation*.

A particularly radical but much needed way of organizing the economy, taking account of the whole, is to arrange society as a trinity in its three functional spheres.[38] The essential idea of a trinity is that paradoxically it is both three and One at the same time. In such an arrangement, the three essential spheres of society: *culture*, the *legal state*, and the *economy* retain independence within their own sphere, but interrelate within the whole.

Each sphere is then able to operate according to its own guiding principles without unnecessarily intruding on the operation of the other spheres except, for example, where guidance is needed from the *cultural sphere* to keep the economy aligned with human purpose. Such an arrangement allows human labour to be removed from the economy as a *commodity* and regulated by contracts agreed in the *legal sphere*. The point of such radical reorganization of a community is to avoid undue dominance of one sphere over another to the detriment of the whole. Each sphere is a field of activity in its own right with its own character and requires independence if total *harmony* is to be achieved. This is another example of the part functioning in relation to the harmony of the whole. The modern values promoted in the French Revolution apply here not in a single synthesis but each within the particular sphere of their utility: *freedom* within culture, *equality* in the legal sphere, and *mutuality* in the economy.

This threefold arrangement of the *social organism* could extend to regions where viable and then spread by example if positive results become evident.[39] There is a tendency already towards separation between these three spheres but the problem at present is that the cultural sphere (where freedom is vital, particularly in the fields of education and religion) is dominated by economic and political concerns, and the economy is therefore unable to function according to purely economic considerations. The political state is also subject to enormous pressure from the economic sphere, so this arrangement of the whole as a trinity enables each part to be autonomous while contributing in a mysterious way to the purpose of the whole, which is the *social organism*. One presumes that this arrangement based on a divine pattern is something of which Boethius would have approved on philosophical and moral grounds had he been alive today. The point here is that consciousness evolves and it is *imperative* that social forms adjust to accommodate the development of human needs, such as liberty, equality, and friendship.

Notes

1 Arthur Manfred Max Neef (1932–2019) was a Chilean economist. Manfred Max Neef's fundamental human needs: wikipedia.org.

2 Cf. Plato's *Republic* 442a & f. The very word 'good' suggests that Boethius accepts an objective hierarchy of values.

3 Philip Mirowski, *Never Let a Serious Crisis go to Waste: How Neoliberalsim Survived the Financial Crisis*. London: Verso, 2014.

4 Macmurray expressed the view that science supplies intellectual and systematic information about the world, but religion reaches up to the full reality of knowledge, to the knowledge of God as the unity of the whole, and as the absolute of personality, God makes knowledge real because God is individual and concrete (Macmurray, 1935/1962: 115–116).

5 Boethius witnesses to those values with his readiness to die. Witness – in Greek: *martyr*; in the diocese of Pavia Boethius was revered as martyr with his feast on 23 October. Cf. B. Watkins, *The Book of Saints: A Comprehensive Biographical Dictionary*, 8th ed. London: Bloomsbury 2016, 108.
6 Cf. (Bukała, 2014). *Risk and Medieval Negotium: Studies of the Attitude Towards Entrepreneurship from Peter the Chanter to Clarus Florentinus*. Spoleto: Fondazione Centro italiano di studi sull'alto Medioevo.
7 That is why Mendicants (Franciscan and Dominicans) with their rejection of every property, were regarded as revolted spirits.
8 Building, Dwelling, Thinking (Heidegger, 1975/2001: 148–149).
9 Mens (mind), spiritus: it is *nous*. Bothius' Platonism is mediated through Neoplatonism. Plotinus speaks about three men in us.
10 This is the Pauline opposition between body – *sarks* and spirit – *pneuma*. Cf. Galatians 5:16–18; Romans 8: 5–6.
11 This harmony could be described in the language of mathematics.
12 It is likely that as a Christian Boethius cannot deprive the material world of any value, and that is why ultimately he refuses to enter the Platonic way of transcendence.
13 From the Christian perspective evil is real but not substantial. St. Augustine (a Manichean lecturer for ten years) discovered this truth in Neoplatonic thought. Manicheans regarded reality as a field of battle between two substances, while St. Augustine proposed a so-called privative idea of evil: evil is a lack (*privatio*) of suitable good. Cf. St. Augustine, *Confessions* VII, 12.
14 This is clearly the influence of Plato's *Gorgias* 466f. This is a very important feature of the Christian idea of evil: evil has no substance but it is a kind of lack of suitable good. When we claim that evil is real without this proviso, we are confronting Manichean dualism: reality comprises two substances: the good and the evil.
15 Cf. Plato's myth about heavenly and earthly Aphrodite in the *Symposium* 180d–182a.
16 This seems to corroborate the idea of Oikos as the well-balanced soul. Agamben discusses in *Kingdom and the Glory* the proto-Christian community's understanding of the 'economy of the mystery' (how the holy spirit comes into human being) but also 'the mystery of the economy'. It seems that Oikos is this place of balancing and mingling between Being and beings or Being as becoming.
17 This is exactly the idea of *musica mundana* and *humana* from Boethius, *De institutione musica 1, 2*, ed. G. Friedlein, Leipzig 1867, 187.
18 Buddhist Economics: wikipedia.org.
19 This is an echo of the Stoic distinction between those things which 'depend on us' (inner goods) and those that do not depend on us. Cf. Epictetus, *The Discourses of Epictetus: With the Encheiridion and Fragments*. London: Bell, 1912, I, 1.
20 These were first called the 'Seven Liberal Arts' during the medieval age. The first three, the Trivium, laid the foundation for the other four arts, which Boethius knew as the Quadrivium.
21 Cf. (Chantal, 2006). *The Unlearned Lessons of the Twentieth Century*. This is an important book written by a contemporary philosopher who claims that the only way to keep the idea of human dignity indisputable is to regard the human as an image of God.
22 Cf. Alisdair MacIntyre, *After Virtue*. London: Duckworth, 1981.

23 Aristotle says that a fair description of the Chief Good is that which all things aim at (*The Nicomachean Ethics*, New York: Oxford University Press, 2009, 1094a). Proverbs 29:18: Where there is no vision the people perish.
24 Yanis Varoufakis, *Talking to My Daughter About the Economy*. London: Bodley Head, 2017, 180. Democratization is suggested by Yanis Varoufakis and others, including Quakers.
25 Peter Kropotkin spoke of work as wholly conducted through mutual aid and agreement by volunteers organized in committees and local groups (Kropotkin, 1892/2015: 129–130).
26 This is the thesis of Owen Barfield's book: *Saving the Appearances*.
27 This is the Stoic idea of Nature as dynamic, alive, and rational, with a teleological principle.
28 This bridging of the subject-object divide by imagination can be achieved by imagining the complete development of a plant from seed to flower so that the sequence of forms conveys the formative movement. In this way, the formative forces are experienced. By means of this active phenomenological method Goethe was able to visualize the archetype applicable to all plants. Rudolf Steiner commented that because one spirit works both in nature and in man's inner life, a person is able to lift their self to participation in the productions of nature (Steiner, 1985: 59).
29 Cf. Plato, *Timaeus* 35a–35b.
30 33. The Labour Party published a report in 2019 titled: *Land for the Many*. Writing about this in *The Guardian* on 4 June 2019, George Manbiot highlighted the need for a change in land ownership to tackle inequality due to the inequitable financial advantage land ownership confers with its inflated financial value.
31 In his introduction to the Enneads of Plotinus, Paul Henry says that for Plotinus the One is alone the Absolute, but the attributes which Christianity confers on its Triune God with three equal persons, are distributed by Plotinus among three hypostases which are distinct and unequal: the *One* as the source of all things, the *Intellect* as the seat of self-thought within the unending Ideas, and the *Soul* of the world as the seat of Providence (Plotinus, 1956: xliv).
32 Biodynamic agriculture is traditional organic agriculture but follows the coordination between nature and the cosmos for harnessing of the dynamic energies of life. See Biodynamic Agriculture: www.wikipedia.org.
33 An echo of this is to be found in William Blake's *Jerusalem* (Blake, 2000) where Jesus is the body in which everything is contained but also is a character within the 'self-contained' whole.
34 Knowledge plays a very important part in human free choice. *Iudicium* is – according to Boethius – an important element of *liberum arbitrium*. So we can say that freedom grows as our knowledge grows.
35 www.sekem.com.
36 For modern economics, land is a common pool resource, like air or water; therefore, a key political task is to democratically agree rules for land governance and its allocation and use, possibly through planning, regulation, and taxation systems (Large and Briault, 2018: 171).
37 In his essay, 'Transforming the Economy', Peter Bowman argues that the effect of de-commoditized credit directed toward productive economic activity, and de-commoditized land freed from speculative valuation, and taxation removed from production would impact on economic activity to create the possibility for self-employment and meaningful work so that bargaining power could shift from employer to employee (Lorimer, 2010: 257–258).

38 This is proposed in *Towards Social Renewal*, by Rudolf Steiner. See 'Social Threefolding': Wikipedia.com.

39 Sekem is a holistic sustainable development in Egypt based on *Threefolding*, intended to develop the individual, society, and the environment through a holistic conception that integrates economic, societal, and cultural life (Large and Briault, 2018: 139).

References

Agamben, Georgio (2011). *Kingdom and the Glory: For a Theological Genealogy of Economy and Government*. Stanford, CA: Stanford University Press.

Aristotle (2009). *The Nicomachean Ethics*. New York: Oxford University Press.

Augustine of Hippo Saint (1970). *The Confessions of St Augustine*. London: Dent.

Barfield, Owen (1957/1988). *Saving the Appearances*. New Hampshire: Wesleyan University Press.

Blake, William (2000). *The Complete Illuminated Books*. London: Thames and Hudson.

Boethius (1867). *De institutione musica 1, 2*. Edited by G. Friedlein. Leipzig.

Boethius (2014). *Consolatio Philosophiae*. Edited by Peter Snipes. Open Source Classics. Chicago: Pluteo Pleno.

Bukała, Marcin (2014). *Risk and Medieval Negotium: Studies of the Attitude Towards Entrepreneurship from Peter the Chanter to Clarus Florentinus*. Spoleto: Fondazione Centro italiano di studi sull'alto Medioevo.

Cadman, David (2010). *A Way of Being*. Suffolk: Zig Publishing.

Delsoi, Chantel (2006). *The Unlearned Lessons of the Twentieth Century*. Wilmington, DL: I S I Books.

Eisenstein, Charles (2011). *Sacred Economics*. Berkeley, CA: North Atlantic Books.

Epictetus (1912). *The Discourses of Epictetus: With the Encheiridion and Fragments*. London: Bell.

Fromm, Erich (1994). *On Being Human*. New York: Continuum.

George, Henry (1879/1976). *Progress and Poverty*. London: Dent.

Georgescu-Roegen, Nicholas (1971). *The Entropy Law and the Economic Process*. Cambridge, MA: Harvard University Press.

Heidegger, Martin (1975/2001). *Poetry, Language, Thought*. New York: Perennial Classics, Harper-Collins.

HRH The Prince of Wales; Juniper, Tony and Skelly, Ian, (2019). *Harmony, a New Way of Looking at Our World*. London: Harper-Collins.

Kapp, William K. (1985). *The Humanization of the Social Sciences*. London: University Press of America.

Ker, W.P. (1923/1955). *The Dark Ages*. London: Thomas Nelson & Sons.

Kropotkin, Peter (1892/2015). *The Conquest of Bread*. London: Penguin Classics.

Kumar, Satish (2019). *Elegant Simplicity*. Gabriola, BC: New Society Publishers.

Large, Martin and Briault, Steve, editors (2018). *Free, Equal and Mutual: Rebalancing Society for the Common Good*. Gloucestershire: Hawthorn Press.

Lewis, C.S. (1943/1962). *The Abolition of Man*. London: Geoffrey Bles.

Lorimer, David, editor (2010). *A New Renaissance*. Edinburgh: Floris Books.
MacIntyre, Alasdair C. (1981). *After Virtue*. London: Duckworth.
Macmurray, John (1935/1962). *Reason and Emotion*. London: Faber and Faber.
Mearman Andrew: Berger, Sebastian and Guizzo, Danielle, editors (2019). *What Is Heterodox Economics: Interviews with Leading Economists*. London: Routledge.
Milne, Joseph (2013). *The Mystical Cosmos*. London: Temenos Academy.
Mirowski, Philip (2014). *Never Let a Serious Crisis Go to Waste: How Neoliberalism Survived the Financial Crisis*. London: Verso.
New Testament Bible. (1946). New York, Glasgow and Toronto: Collins.
Nishida, Kitaro (1949/1993). *Last Writings, Nothingness and the Religious Worldview*. Honolulu: University of Hawaii Press.
Plato (1971). *Gorgias*. Harmondsworth: Penguin Books.
Plato (2004). *Symposium*. Oxford and New York: Oxford University Press.
Plato (2007). *The Republic*. London: Penguin Books.
Plato (2015). *Laws*. Oxford: Oxford University Press.
Plotinus (1948). *The Essence of Plotinus*. Compiled by G.H. Turnbull. New York: Oxford University Press.
Plotinus (1956). *The Enneads*. Translated by Stephen MacKenna. London: Faber and Faber.
Schumacher, Ernst (1973). *Small Is Beautiful: A Study of Economics as if People Mattered*. London: Blond and Briggs.
Sedlacek, Tomas (2011/2013). *Economics of Good and Evil*. New York: Oxford University Press, Inc.
Steiner, Rudolf (1985). *Goethe's World View*. New York: Mercury Press.
Steiner, Rudolf (1977). *Towards Social Renewal*. London: Rudolf Steiner Press.
Tillich, Paul (1957). *Systematic Theology*, vol. 2. London: James Nisbet.
Varoufakis, Yanis (2017). *Talking to My Daughter About the Economy*. London: Bodley Head.
Watkins, B., editor (2016). *The Book of Saints: A Comprehensive Biographical Dictionary*. London: Bloomsbury.

5 Conclusion

The following ten key insights support re-rooting economics in the human soul where a poetic-philosophic economy delivers consolation and fruition.

Key Insights

Poetic-Philosophic Economy	Modern Economics
1. Seat of Truth	1. Truth as market calculus
2. Justice	2. Luck and chance
3. Inner wealth	3. Outer possessions
4. Being	4. Having
5. Basic needs	5. Consumerism
6. Self-sufficiency	6. Insatiability
7. Circulation	7. Hoarding
8. Fruition	8. Progress
9. Goodness from higher nature	9. Egoism
10. Freedom as self-sufficiency	10. Freedom of choice in markets

1. **Seat of Truth versus Truth as market calculus**: Being, Knowledge, and Goodness are united in the whole, and the purpose of knowledge is to come into accord with the Truth of things in thought and action (Milne, 2013: 12). The oikos takes on the attributes of the whole where philosophy's embodied knowledge as wisdom, and the power of logic, reason, and intuition, come into play. This is a major contrast to modern economics' reduction of knowledge to an algorithm of calculation.
2. **Justice versus Luck and chance**: Justice in the oikos is other-worldly, governed by Providence as Divine Mind, whereas worldly luck and chance are governed by Fate as the order of things subject to change. A self-sufficient oikos is a just economy because it meets all relevant needs, but an economy subject to luck and chance is unpredictable and

DOI: 10.4324/9781003226093-5

incomplete, producing the chance of riches for some but accompanied by adversity and crises. The discrepancy between the harmonious rule of the Heavens and Fortune's sublunary dominance within time gives scope for *progression*, but for *Consolation* positive progress lies in self-mastery and virtuous participation in the Good, not in the multiplication of consumer goods.

3. **Inner wealth versus Outer possessions**: Inner wealth is found in the soul or Self. Inner wealth is 'embodied' and cannot be easily stolen as with outer possessions. This is a question of where a person's attention is directed. A person's destiny is affected in the choice between cultivating inner wealth or outer possessions. True wealth lies in cultivation of a rich inner life accompanied by virtue, which includes self-control, and pursuit of the Good. The result of this is True happiness in distinction to the materialistic concern for accumulation of material possessions. The importance of Inner wealth lies in its connection to the transcendental. It is inner wealth to know that you are made in the image of God, but the *virtue ethics* of oikos has to be distinguished from the neoclassical *decision ethic* of utility maximization.
4. **Being versus Having**: Worldviews and attitudes that shape one's relationship to reality have their impact on the economy. The distinction between *Being* and *Having* alerts us to the danger of forgetfulness of Being. Ownership of things can so occupy a person's attention that 'Being', as participation in the Good, gets overlooked as a personal concern. On the other hand the soul, as oikos, celebrates participation in transcendental completion. Unlike 'having', 'being' is free from the fear of loss. But as a *verb*, Being cannot be known in the same way that an object (as a noun) is known. The experience of Being requires participation, surrender, and commitment. Here, an I–Thou relationship is appropriate for Being and Nature. And again, this I–Thou relationship applies in the oikos, but modern economics employs the I–It relationship turning the Good into 'goods'.
5. **Basic Needs versus Consumerism**: The distinction between an oikos that serves basic needs and an economy driven by consumerism is connected to the distinction between 'being' and 'having'. The distinction concerns the metaphysical question of the aspiration and orientation of the heart (soul), which relates to the fundamental question of the meaning and purpose of life. The oikos represents self-sufficiency in connection with Being, while the materialist motive evident in consumerism essentially focuses human concern on the sense-world. When this motive dominates, arguably according to *Consolation*, it represents the reduction of the human to the animal. Here, Darwinian Man loses conscious connection to a Divine origin. Material poverty can

in fact be chosen by someone dedicated to spiritual activity and service to humanity, as a way of avoiding distractions from sense-bound possessions.

6. **Self-sufficiency versus Insatiability**: The oikos as soul is self-sufficient through its connection to the Good, which is the whole, and Nature represents the Good in providing raw materials as substance for the economy. However, Nature is an entire living system so demands an I–Thou relationship. This calls for caring and sustainable methods of agriculture, farming, and manufacture. Growth in an *organic* manner is a characteristic of living nature, for which the modern economy substitutes *continuous* growth, but this overlooks the fact that nature has a life cycle of birth, development, and decay. This miss-match between nature and mechanistic thinking and practice causes economic instability. The abstract, calculative thinking of modern economics is out of step with Nature in this respect, and its methods, including heavily industrialized farming, are unsuited to a living system. Again this miss-match causes environmental damage leading to instability. The assumption of infinite growth in Gross National Product as a measure of an economy is unworkable in a finite world. A more appropriate, stable, and sustainable measure would be the Index of Sustainable Economic Welfare (IOSEW) or Gross National Happiness (GNH).
7. **Circulation versus Hoarding**: The contrast between circulation and hoarding highlights the difference between *oikos* and *chremastistics*. Based on the soul, the oikos is alive (organic) and responsive, with all of its elements interconnected. This living quality enables flow and interconnectivity to thrive. The oikos exists essentially in its connections, and hoarding interrupts this flow. Hoarding happens within wealth-creating modern economics because the system itself encourages acquisitiveness. The motive for Hoarding would be better directed towards investment in the real economy.
8. **Fruition versus Progress**: Fruition is the ability to live a complete and flourishing life in the present where a person's divine and personal potential can be realized. Eternity can exert an influence on daily life when there is consciousness of the immanence of Being (of God and the Good). The possibility exists for grasping eternal life in its immediacy in our lives; this is fruition. Recognition of a divine Creator of Nature (the cosmos) and Humanity is the foundation for transcendental union and spiritual welfare. The focus for this is the oikos where time produces *qualitative value* in its relation to the eternal. Progress, as a modern concept, is an experience and measure of time as linear, quantitative, and mathematical rather than a *qualitative* experience. Fruition

is fullness, while progress in the modern sense is abstract, lacking in value, and even regressive in terms of human values.

9. **Goodness from higher nature versus Egoism**: A moral question arises when we are told that Goodness comes into being through participation in the Good. Wickedness departs from the Good and the destination of each direction is different: Goodness towards divinity and wickedness towards an animal nature. The ego has a vital and necessary human function but it is problematic in that it includes within it a higher and a lower aspect as a result of its interface between the divine spirit and the animal body. Aspiration towards the Good engages the 'higher', while egoism (as love and care primarily for oneself) involves the 'lower' aspect of the ego. The ego (or the 'I' as *spirit within the soul*) is the stage on which the dramatic conflict between good and evil is enacted. In this sense, the *Consolation* presents the drama of Boethuis' ego. Adoption of the oikos in the medieval period produced a particularly stable kind of society, and similarly the modern economy in turn determines a particular form of society. But what is at stake in the distinction between goodness and egoism is *Being*, because the soul, as oikos (the ego is included within the soul), is also the earthly household enlivened by Goodness, which is key to a fruitful relationship to the reality of Being. The fact of evil in a world governed by the Good is problematic for Boethius, which is why *Consolation* can also be taken as a theodicy that justifies God's sovereignty over a world of suffering and evil. The insight that Boethius contributes is to say that Providence presides over Fate as the necessity behind change within time. Providence represents the oikos opening to Being where a basic oikos provides material support without offering undue temptation for egoism. A society focused on the Good will experience the positive impacts of cooperation, friendship, and harmony. Love is needed to rule not only the heart but also the economy. Indeed, such a need is taken up by Feminist Economics with its emphasis on the economic significance of care in the household. Equally Ecological Economics demonstrates a caring attitude to the environment, and Green Economics cares for the economy as a component part within the ecosystem in which it is embedded. Here, the reverent I–Thou attitude to nature is vital.
10. **Freedom as self-sufficiency versus Freedom of choice in markets**: Boethius believed that a person was most free when contemplating the Mind of God and when pursuing the path of Goodness. Consequently, such a person would be in a right relationship to reality. Such a relationship represents self-sufficiency, opening to the Whole. Freedom involves breaking away from the egocentric cage of selfish desire.

> When given up to wickedness (departure from Goodness) a person is not free, but bound by the 'wickedness'. Providence provides freedom in the oikos, but Fortune governs freedom of choice in markets, giving rise to uncertainty because of incompleteness. Freedom, a key concern in our time, is addressed by the threefold arrangement of society where culture, the economy, and legal government retain individual autonomy yet intercommunicate and interact for the benefit of the whole social organism without one of the three spheres oppressing the others. Freedom arises in the cultural sphere when it is not dominated by economics or by the legal state. In meeting basic needs in the economy, the oikos enables freedom through self-sufficiency, while the market of supposed freedom of choice is subject to instability because of its subjection to the 'Wheel of Fortune'. The supposed freedom of choice offered by the market can, through advertising, compel people, and it tends to ignore what it excludes, chief of which is morality, cohesion, and the well-being of society as a whole.

The fundamental distinction listed here between an ancient classical worldview and modernity raises the question of the relation of a worldview to knowledge. Modernity reduces all orders of knowledge to the single dimension of the scientific reasoning, but this viewpoint is linear and exclusive. Unlike ancient classical and poetic knowledge, it cannot relate epistemologically to the metaphysical dimension of ontology. Philosophy takes cognizance of the *soul* in that the human being can be considered as a 'being there' for Being. The soul responds to different levels or orders of being: to the Divine (theology), to the nature of Being (philosophy as metaphysics), and to natural existence (Nature or physics), and likewise the oikos takes account of the divine as well as the earthly practicalities of existence. Philosophy (as metaphysics) is the engine for reflection on the source, the end, and the means. From an ancient perspective, the Good is central. Consequently within *Consolation*, the oikos plays a significant role in the context of the meaning of life's journey.

Boethius was a dedicated scholar of classical philosophy and literature, a translator, and a Christian, so his evaluation of life, written while under sentence of death, provides a profound and deeply felt foundation for rethinking economics as an economy made for humanity and not a humanity made for the economy. In this respect, a person is understood as 'made in the image of God'. *Consolation* challenges us to ask whether or not today we have forgotten our true nature and are therefore homeless, without a meaningful direction, individually and as a society. In this respect, *Consolation* presents us with the timeless ideal of the Good and the rule of love in human hearts

(Boethius, 1999: 28–30). Ancient philosophy speaks of love as the binding force that holds all together, yet it also recognizes the necessity of strife in the maintenance of life. But Love is stronger, otherwise strife would lead to chaos. In fact, we have now reached a stage in human development requiring the activation of love to contain strife leading to chaos.

Love, from a Christian perspective, is in fact a divine power intended to rule in the human heart. It acts in the interest and care for the whole, which is precisely what Pope Francis argued for in his Encyclical of 2015. This document, titled *Care for our Common Home*, is addressed to all people of good will. In it, Pope Francis refers to the scientific method as 'a technique of possession', and that this alerts us to a need for change in the 'epistemological paradigm' that has now become globalized. The 'myth of modernity' is described as a utilitarian mindset of individualism, unlimited progress, competition, consumerism, and an unregulated market. On the other hand, wisdom is described as the fruit of self-examination, dialogue, and generous encounter between persons. It is said that what is needed to confront today's issues is a science that takes account of data generated by other fields of knowledge, including philosophy and social ethics, and that environmental education should acknowledge the transcendent in order to give the deepest meaning to ecological ethics. As such, the Encyclical affirms the contemporary relevance of Boethius' consoling philosophy.

Although an ancient worldview based on a divine foundation has been eclipsed in the West, this can be seen as the necessity of Fate as it unwinds in the process of the evolution of human consciousness. In this respect, it is interesting to note how Nominalism eclipsed Realism in the late medieval period: where once a *concept* of the Divine was taken to be reality and then the concept became a mere name. Arguably the effect of this cultural reorientation in adopting Nominalism has led to denial of *reality* to the divine, as well as a materialistic foundation for science, with its consequent reduction of human awareness to a merely material world. But a phase of materialism can be seen to have its rightful place within the scope of Providence (within an evolution of consciousness), yet when it persists (due to inertia) beyond its useful time, it can have evil effects. Indeed, the neoliberal economics of modernity now clearly demonstrate a tendency to destroy lives and the environment to an extent that defies logic. If the lived experience of the metaphysical (spiritual) and natural world presented by Boethius had continued without interruption, it is conceivable that a science and technology would have developed in sympathy with this, and instead of deploying destructive techniques of control, there would be cooperation with nature and its energies – an approach acknowledging the sacredness of nature and the economic advantage of working with rather than against the direction of living nature.

With regard to the question of growth and sustainability, what is needed is an increase in ethical awareness, to allow the oikos of *Consolation* to be viewed in a positive light, in its contrast with the neoliberal growth economy that, in a finite world, risks destabilizing civilization and life. In the interests of the future of the individual and the community, a growing awareness of ecological connectedness and the sanctity of life is vital. But for change to happen on a large scale, a supportive critical mass from civil society and the community is needed so that initiatives can be undertaken at a local level and beyond. Institutions have their place and can encourage participation through communicating relevant ideas; one of particular relevance is the *New Economics Foundation*,[1] which appears to share Boethius' human values. As W. P. Ker remarked, Boethius not only had introduced the course of medieval speculation, he transcended it, and his doctrine remains fresh as an indisputable perennial source of moral wisdom (Ker, 1955: 40). Since the present concern for the welfare of the planet calls urgently for a fresh attitude to the world, this is where *Consolation* becomes actively relevant with its contribution of ancient wisdom informing a perennial philosophy that has long been disregarded by modernity. An evolution of consciousness may change our perception of the world but it is arguable if it substantially changes essential reality. This is where Being and becoming connect and reveal the pressing need for humanity to regain awareness of the divine, which can reassert the relevance of morality in human life and aid it in flourishing.

Long-lived societies have been characterized by unity of vision and there is potential today for a universal vision that respects the human being. United Nations declarations point in this direction, particularly concerning universal human rights. What is required to underpin universal ethics is a foundational 'perennial philosophy' that combines ancient wisdom with religious, moral, ethical, and modern insights to provide a flexible structure. It is to such a non-dogmatic vision that the philosophy of Boethius contributes. This represents a dramatic contrast to a modern science-based, materialist paradigm. But bearing in mind an evolution in consciousness, it is important to see Boethius in his historical context as a lover of ancient wisdom from his sixth-century vantage point in a household and empire observant of Christianity. So the oikos within the *Consolation* must be seen in the context of an awareness of the significance of God as the Creative Power in and behind the universe. It is in this, and particularly from ancient philosophy, that Boethius' derived his concern for a rightful relationship to reality. Seen in this light, the inspired synthesis of knowledge and wisdom distilled in *Consolation* still today presents a compelling argument for re-rooting the economy in oikos.

Boethius' worldview embodies universal values in the morality that it advocates and in the wisdom and poetry and religious conception to which he devoted himself, and *Consolation* directs our attention to the vitally important human concerns of morality, conscience, and the idea that knowledge depends upon the ability of the knower to know. In the light of this perennial wisdom, we need to ask whether or not humanity still has a purpose, and if so what that purpose is, and whether the economy at present hinders or helps in this. W. P. Ker reminds us of the ancient idea that the goodness of the human being is seen to maintain the universe. From a divine perspective, morality is objective, and divinely inspired love is a power capable of enabling communion and providing connection between an individual and Nature and an individual and the community. Herein lies Goodness. The alternative appears to be alienation leading to destruction.

Karl Polyani penetrated to the heart of the problem posed by modern economics when he said that if industrialism is not to extinguish the race it must be subordinated to the requirements of man's nature. For Polyani, the true criticism of a market society was not that it is based on economics but that its economy is based on self-interest (Polanyi, 2001: 257). In this respect, it is important to note that Natural Law promotes the idea of fulfilment of individual potential so as to contribute to the whole, the Good, but on the contrary, actualization of self-interest results in separation from the whole, and alienation (Milne, 2008: 63). Polanyi also remarked on the fact that Jowett had failed to see that the distinction between the principle of *use* and *gain* was key to the utterly different civilizations, which Aristotle accurately forecast 2,000 years before its advent (Polanyi, 2001: 57). In his essay, 'Transforming the Economy', Peter Bowman refers to Polyanyi's ideas and suggests that the way to eliminate the negative impacts of the current financial system on the environment and human welfare is to decommoditize labour, land, and credit, by removing them from the economic equation so that these can relate effectively to the 'needs economy' of the oikos where credit is directed to production of goods, land is evaluated so that its use-value can be taxed (alleviating tax on labour), and labour is freed from compulsion (Lorimer, 2010: 254).

A radical arrangement for meeting today's evolutionary need for *individual freedom* within a *healthy commons* is tri-formation of society. This model pictures a triangular arrangement of the sector of politics, culture, and the economy, enclosed within the circle of society so that the focal points of triangle and circle converge. Reshaping society in this 'mysterious' way restricts each sector to its own sphere so as to achieve overall social harmony. But the introduction of such a model calls for inner human change consistent with participation in the Good: what might be called a 'new way of being'. The vision (worldview) adopted by an era decides its economy, and while we live in a highly technical civilization, we must not forget that ultimately the economy is a result not only of the resources available, but also of human decision and vision. David Cadman reminds us that if we want change we must replace the old language with a new language, and that this can only be done if we change our way of being in a way connected to teachings in the realm of divine discourse (Cadman, 2010: 45). Indeed the cognition of the classical (and medieval) world, that Boethius represents, was open to the transcendental and concerned for a just relationship to reality, whereas modernity wilfully objectifies in order to control.

A crisis such as a global pandemic illuminates the relationship between health and the economy. This largely concerns physical health within a material economy, but Boethius' medical metaphor, which relates to health of the spirit, is relevant and vital for economics concerned with *care of the soul*. The oikos is the household of the soul where the immaterial and the material meet,[2] and *Consolation* presents a philosophy where the oikos (as soul) is the living bridge between the divine and the earthly. Speaking of this living nature of the economy with its flow and distribution, Owen Barfield observed the need for a living approach to be applied in the thinking of the economy, where the 'living' quality in art can cooperate with the 'dead' (mechanistic) thinking of science (Barfield, 1999: 150), and Richard Tonas speaks of the need for a new paradigm equivalent to a new Copernican revolution but that this is held back for the lack of a 'coherent cosmology'.[3]

Speaking of the Copernican revolution, in his book *Saving the Appearances*, Owen Barfield argued that what is needed today in order to set in motion a post-modern enlightenment, is a new kind of participation that involves a re-awakened awareness of the divine – not as faith but as knowledge (Barfield, 1957/1988: 157–158). The appropriate new 'paradigm' must involve renewal of awareness of the Divine within. This means awareness of the inwardness of the divine presence (being made in the image of God), the 'I AM' in the soul, and so in the oikos. Participation in Nature and the Divine is achieved by cultivating the divine seed within to experience (as it were through divine eyes) the 'livingness' of Nature and Being. This mode of participation is a direct contrast to what Barfield called the idolatry of seeing things as completely separate from our own cognition, and as a result feeling alienated from these appearances.

If we understand the substance of the universe as embodying the Divine (or is Divine embodiment), this means that substance is informed by Divine Mind. This ancient classical understanding reveals an *awareness* that we could regain today with its corollary of human access to cosmic intelligence. We need to re-cognize Nature and its denizens as the Creation of Divine Intelligence, and to see Creation as an evolutionary process in continuous movement. Addressing this question, David Fideler speaks of the future-oriented work of John Todd as a new alchemy that involves cooperating with the intelligence in Nature; for example, using bacteria and other organisms to purify water. This is an approach that respects the living genius of Nature, which exceeds current human intelligence because it is informed by cosmic intelligence (Fideler, 2014: 241). Max Payne even argues that advances in science will actually reveal the falseness of Materialist Reductionism and that rather than Mind being seen as an epiphenomenon of the brain, Mind (as consciousness) will be recognized as the source of the phenomenon of matter, and this will be the *hinge* on which a new renaissance turns. Materialist Reductionism will then no longer be scientifically, philosophically, or logically valid and this reversal will inaugurate a new spiritual era, more of existential wonder and engagement than of dogma (Payne in Lorimer, 2010: 194).

Philosophia presents the homeland of the soul as a region of conflict between virtue and vice in which the virtuous oikos is characterized by completeness containing a *living* organic quality that responds directly to needs. Such an oikos supports goodness, which upholds the universe, because pursuit of the Good orientates humanity towards reality, aligning the human with divine-cosmic purpose. An oikos of consolation that recognizes human and divine purpose makes its appeal to the logic of the head and the feeling heart, to the intellect and to the conscience through which objective morality arises. This is where the human spirit–soul connects with the divine in meaningful evolutionary purpose. When we ask ourselves what is at stake today, we find essentially two orientations of knowledge and belief: love/egoism, life/mechanization, communion/separation, truth/deception, beauty/ugliness, and goodness/evil. The first perspective is informed by the transcendental (by a conception of a divinely created living cosmos), and the other by a historically conditioned human view set within the limits of materialism. The Platonic view favours the former, and Boethius' cure (consolation) conducted by Philosophia, works on the premise that knowledge is recollection. To restrict knowledge merely to what is rational and empirical is to ignore other rich sources; it is to accept insufficiency in relation to the whole while ignoring the possibility that there could be more than is dreamed of in a single (one-sided) philosophy.

Ancient philosophy was *a way of life* as distinct from the theoretical and speculative philosophy of today. In ancient philosophy, the self was situated in the cosmic whole, unlike the situation today where the self is alienated from the environment, and theory and pragmatism tend to replace the desire for wisdom as lived experience. What modernity has lost, with its egocentric focus, is the experience of connection within cosmic nature as an active process: as the experience of living within the movement of life as a part within the whole, with consciousness as the link. Pierre Hadot remarks that to understand the meaning of old truths they have to be lived (Hadot, 1995: 108). So it is important to understand the *living* quality of the oikos as soul. This is the living quality of connectedness of living nature pervaded by spirit.

Boethius refers to wholeness as the Good, and deviation from this as sickness in need of healing (making whole). Since the link between life and economics is direct this medical metaphor is useful. Healthy, or abundant life, is connected to universality (the unity of oneness) which implies mutuality. Opposing this is the egocentric self that seeks the power of dominance, exploitation, and exclusivity that pits the part against the welfare of the whole. Today, the hinge between health promotion and procedures toxic to life turns on the financial (wealth creation) sector where it is a question of orientation: directing this potential either to life or to the elimination of life. An existential threat exists to the whole (the divine that embraces the cosmos, humankind, and the earth's living ecosystems); human orientation is balanced on the knife-edge of whether to affirm life or pursue practices and technologies hostile to wholesome and abundant life.

There is a pressing need for holism; for reconciling our two modes of cognition, our inner Plato (artist) and inner Aristotle (scientist), in the manner of Boethius' *Consolation*. An inner Copernican revolution will involve growing awareness of the inner I-AM, the divine in the soul and the oikos. This implies the knowledge that our consciousness participates in what we perceive. Our mode of thinking impacts on cognition, and in recognizing this, we need a new renaissance based on the holism of science (mind), art (heart-soul), and religion (spirit). What Nature cries out for is revitalized human cognition: re-cognition of human nature with its relation to Nature and the Divine. Here, Truth is the original source and ground of being that is mysteriously accessible within the soul. Given such a new renaissance, an appropriate economy will follow. Taking the long view, with each new generation arises the possibility of commitment to a fresh vision. Change is constant on the Wheel of Fate that turns under the guidance of Providence.

Notes

1 New Economics Foundation: www.wikipedia.org.
2 Boethius' accepted Aristotle's definition of man as a 'rational and moral animal' (Boethius, 1999: 20, 8–9). Rationality as a quality of soul is spiritual, and the home of the 'animal' is the material earth. This qualifies the identity of the human person as soul, and the *oikos* as the earthly dwelling place, and this relationship of the rational to the animal has consequences for the human economy. 'Contra Eutychen et Nestorium' in *Theological Tractates* contains a famous Boethian definition of a person: 'rationalis naturae individua (individual/non divided) substantia'.
3 'The Greater Copernican Revolution and the Crisis of the Modern World View' (Lorimer, 2010: 50).

References

Barfield, Owen (1957/1988). *Saving the Appearances: A Study in Idolatry*. New Hampshire: Wesleyan University Press.

Barfield, Owen (1999). *A Barfield Reader*. Edited by G.B. Tennyson. Edinburgh: Floris Books.

Boethius (1969/1999). *The Consolation of Philosophy*. Translated by Victor Watts. London: Penguin Books.

Cadman, David (2010). *A Way of Being*. Suffolk: Zig Publishing.

Fideler, David (2014). *Restoring the Soul of the World*. Rochester, VT: Inner Traditions.

Hadot, Pierre (1995). *Philosophy as a Way of Life*. Malden, MA: Blackwell Publishing.

Ker, W.P. (1923/1955). *The Dark Ages*. London: Thomas Nelson & Sons.

Milne, Joseph (2008). *Metaphysics and the Cosmic Order*. London: Temenos Academy.

Milne, Joseph (2013). *The Mystical Cosmos*. London: Temenos Academy.

Lorimer, David and Robinson, Oliver, editors (2010). *A New Renaissance: Transforming Science, Spirit and Society*. Edinburgh: Floris Books.

Polanyi, Karl (1944/2001). *The Great Transformation*. Boston: Beacon Press.

Pope Francis (2015). *Care for Our Common Home*. Vatican: Encyclical Letter.

Stewart, H.F. and Rand, E.K. (1968). *The Theological Tractates*. Cambridge, MA: Harvard University Press.

Index

Printed in the United States
by Baker & Taylor Publisher Services